Economics and
Urban Problems

ECONOMICS AND URBAN PROBLEMS

Diagnoses and Prescriptions

SECOND AND ENLARGED EDITION

DICK NETZER

Basic Books, Inc., Publishers • New York

Preface

Until quite recently, economists, like almost everyone else, had seriously neglected the great problems of American urban society. We were preoccupied with other pressing public policy problems—inflation, unemployment, and long-term growth of the American economy; the functioning of the domestic and international monetary system; economic development in the preindustrial countries of the world; competition and concentration in American industry; federal tax policy; and many more. We were also much concerned with the development of analytic tools and systems appropriate to these types of policy issues.

In the 1950s, a few economists addressed themselves to regional and local economic problems within the United States. Our concern stemmed from more traditional "fields" within economics—work on the fiscal problems of local and state governments; analysis of local labor markets and housing markets; interest in interregional movement of labor and capital; and a directly intellectual interest in finding new applications for recently developed analytic tools, for example, input-output analysis. Regional and urban economics rapidly became a distinct field within economics, partly because of the intellectual achievements of regional and urban economists, and even more so because we are all now so self-consciously aware of the gravity of America's urban problems.

This book examines a number of the most serious urban problems from the standpoint of an urban economist. It does not present a systematic exposition of the theoretical tools used in formal urban economic analysis, but instead is problem and policy oriented. The goal is to make an understanding of the application of economics to urban problems accessible to those with limited previous exposure to formal course work in economic analysis, but an effort has been made to use the tools of economics in a reasonably rigorous fashion. Thus, the book should be useful in urban economics courses (presumably, in graduate courses, only when used together with a formal analytic text) as well as in interdisciplinary urban problems courses and as a supplementary text for urban courses in other social science disciplines.

In the four years since the first edition of this book was published, urban problems have not abated, nor have the policy issues been resolved. However, a number of important new policies have been implemented, and new policy issues are now in the public eye. This revised edition reflects these changes; the book has also been updated to incorporate the most recent data available, which is necessary in a rapidly changing world. Also, Chapter 1 has been revised to spell out the basic theoretical setting of urban economics somewhat more completely than was done in the first edition.

I am indebted to numerous urban economists for their comments on the first edition, especially my colleagues at New York University, and to urbanists in Britain, especially those at the Centre for Environmental Studies, where I began work on the revision. Sylvia Curtis was responsible for the lion's share of the typing of the manuscript within an extremely tight deadline.

DICK NETZER

Contents

vii

PART I

THE URBAN SETTING

1

Introduction:
The Urban Economy

The problems of cities are by no means the exclusive preserve of economists. Economics deals with only one "slice of life," and life in cities is so complex that the study of urban problems can be sliced many ways. Economics is concerned with the production of goods and services: which and how many goods and services are produced for people to use; how these goods and services are distributed among people; the processes and institutions through which decisions on production and distribution are reached; and how the processes and the results can be improved. It is, in short, concerned with the "wealth of nations," as the father of economics, Adam Smith, said, and the wealth of parts of nations, including cities and their inhabitants.

We economists base our theoretical systems on the fundamental assumption that the goal of economic activity is an increase in wealth, defined in the very broad sense used by Adam Smith. We are not so naive or arrogant as to believe that an increase in material wealth is what life is all about. The economist's pretensions are more modest: to study how the real resources of a society—its people and their talents, its

3

land, its other natural resources—can be deployed so as to yield the maximum in satisfaction to that society, recognizing that the sources of satisfaction and dissatisfaction are varied indeed and transcend economics. But the level and distribution of real income (that is, income measured in goods and services, rather than in terms of money alone) is not a trivial factor in satisfaction. Low incomes or improper use of real resources, or both, are among the significant contributing factors to most of today's truly important urban social problems. Economists have developed tools of analysis and methods of research which permit them to isolate the economic causes of these problems and to evaluate alternative solutions to these economic causes and the economic consequences of noneconomic causes and solutions. We have standards of comparison and systems of measurement (about which more will be said later in this chapter) for our "slice of life."

It is clear that many of the afflictions of our cities have causes and cures in which the role of economics is small relative to the disciplines directly concerned with attitudes, social behavior, and technology. Racial discrimination and disadvantage are central to the problems of American cities. It is by now evident that economic improvement by itself does not dissolve racial discrimination, and it is almost surely true that racial discrimination imposes economic costs on discriminators as well as on those discriminated against. Rising crime rates and the increasing failures of the criminal justice system occur in the face of economic improvement, not economic deterioration. The increasing difficulty in effectively providing adequate public and quasi-public services is not caused by a refusal to provide large amounts of resources for health care, police protection, environmental control, education, and the like: consider, for example, the failure of big-city school systems to achieve good scholastic attainment among children in poor families despite high expenditure per pupil. Often the difficulties are sociological or political, but sometimes they are technological: for example, inadequate knowledge and mechanisms for air-pollution control.

Although economics may not be central to these problems, there are economic aspects to them that need to be sorted out, if the problems are to be properly diagnosed and appropriate solutions prescribed. It is all too easy to ignore the economic aspects and offer costly or unworkable solutions, or to throw up our hands in despair because we consider a particular social problem to be a reflection of strongly held and therefore unchangeable social attitudes. A good example of this can be found in discussions of the transportation problems of large cities. Popular writers and social critics are fond of describing much of the urban transportation problem—traffic congestion, vast expenditures for highways, and deteriorating public transportation services—as a consequence of the "American's love affair with his automobile." It is true that Americans, like people almost everywhere else in the world, prefer the comfort, convenience, and speed of private automobile transportation above public transportation when they can afford it. But it is not clear that this is solely a reflection of individual preferences shaped by advertising or other common cultural influences. Economists suspect that differences in the transportation costs confronting people significantly influence their choices among different transportation modes. The question can be put this way: suppose that many automobile trips are in fact heavily subsidized, so that the motorists making those trips pay only a small fraction of the costs of the resources involved. Could the "love affair with the automobile" survive if motorists had to pay the full costs?

Moreover, if the sources of the transportation problem are not economic, but rather cultural, then people in many different cultural settings must also be in love with the automobile, for there is relatively more use of the car for commuting to jobs in city centers in Paris and Manchester than there is in Chicago, and more in London than in New York. London's population is about one-tenth smaller than New York's, with average incomes only about half the New York level. Yet there are more private cars registered in London than in New York, and more people use the car to commute to work in the central area of London than do so in New York, even though London has no system of freeways. The relative subsidy to such trips by car in London is even greater than in New York (mainly because cheap parking in the central area is more readily available), thus producing a result economists would predict without resort to cultural explanations.

Urban Economics and Urban Problems

Formal study of the subject called "urban economics" is rather new: the term "urban economics" was not even coined until the late 1950s. However, economists have always been concerned with the economic aspects of problems that exist in cities. In the nineteenth century and the early part of the twentieth century, economists wrote extensively about such issues as housing, social security and welfare systems to cope with poverty, and the financing of local governments.

What is new—what makes up the field called urban economics—is the explicit linking of the study of such problems with the analysis of what can be broadly (and abstractly) described as the "spatial distribution of activities." That abstract description includes two very concrete lines of study. The first is the study of how and why people and economic activities concentrate themselves in urban areas and how and why individual cities grow at different rates. The second is how and why people and economic activities are located *within* a given urban area.

Economists and geographers studying the growth and internal spatial structure of cities have found some trends or regularities that are so general that they can be said to be "laws." The first of these is well known indeed: the long-term and very persistent increase in urbanization that is worldwide, dating in Western countries from the revival of trade and the acceleration of technological advance in the late Middle Ages. The economic advantages of increasing concentration of the population in relatively large urban places have been explored in depth. These advantages have seemed, until quite recently, to be so overwhelming that most governmental efforts to limit the growth of the largest urban areas—as was tried in Britain, France, the USSR, and China—have been to no avail.

A second "law" relates to the pattern of urban area sizes, or the size distribution of cities. It has been observed that in every country there is a sort of triangle of city sizes, with a small number of very large cities at the apex and a large number of small cities at the base. This common observation has been subjected to statistical tests, and what has emerged is a statistical regularity known as the *rank-size* rule, which says that the product of an urban area's size and its ranking among the cities in that country is a constant. That is, the second largest urban area has half the population of the largest one, the third largest has one-third the population of the largest, and so on. More refined statistical testing has questioned whether this distribution holds precisely in all cases, but there is no doubt that the size distribution of cities conforms to a regular pattern similar to the rank-size rule, a pattern that is remarkably like the usual distribution of income among households that bears the name of the Italian economist Vilfredo Pareto. The regularity is so great that urban economists have devoted a good deal of effort to explaining why this should be so; none of the alternative explanations are completely successful.

A third "law" deals with the internal spatial structure of cities. Although in advanced industrial countries there is increasing concentration in the largest urban areas, there is also a marked tendency toward decentralization within these urban areas. This is the phenomenon of suburbanization: the shift of population from the central cities toward the edges of their metropolitan areas and the dispersal of economic activity from its earlier concentration in the downtown central business district and nearby industrial districts to new clusters and scattered locations throughout the metropolitan area.

The nature and severity of most urban economic problems are generally shaped by the first two "laws." That is, the size and growth rate of an urban area are important determinants of income levels and income distributions, the housing stock, land-use patterns, and transportation needs. But the third "law" is truly crucial for a comprehension of urban economic problems. Access to employment opportunities and to improved housing, environmental damages, transportation systems, and the financing of public services are all directly affected by where people live and where economic activity is located within the urban area and by the links between homes, jobs, tax bases, and the like.

Indeed, one could argue that if different classes of people and different types of economic activity were spread uniformly over the urban landscape, we would not confront any of the problems that now seem to be endemic in large cities. There would be no congestion, no massive concentrations of poverty or blocks of slum housing, and no disparities in the ability of communities to finance public services.

The fact is that people and activities are *not* uniformly

dispersed throughout an urban area; instead, the spatial structure of the urban economy is marked by heterogeneity, differentiation, and segregation. There are wide differences in the economic and social characteristics of the small geographic segments that make up the larger urban area. The most important of these differences is the contrast between the high densities, physical decay, and low incomes that are so visible in the inner parts of the older large cities and the low densities, high physical standards, and high incomes that characterize the newer, outer parts. This is, of course, a direct reflection of the powerful decentralizing trend within urban areas.

Economic Factors in Location Decisions

In Chapter 2, we shall explore more fully the decentralizing trend and its concrete causes. At this point, it is worthwhile to consider briefly the theoretical basis for the spatial structure we observe: what are the economic factors that shape the decisions by households and businesses about where in the urban area they locate? In urban economics, as in most fields in economics, there is not universal agreement on any theoretical proposition. Instead, contending theories coexist, not very peaceably. However, there is a dominant theory about intrametropolitan location decisions, a theory that is supported by a good deal of empirical evidence. This is the "trade-off" theory, first formulated in contemporary terms by Edgar M. Hoover.[1]

---

1. Professor Hoover initially expounded the theory in connection with a large-scale study of the economy of the New York metropolitan region, in Edgar M. Hoover and Raymond Vernon, *Anatomy of a Metropolis* (Cambridge, Mass.: Harvard University Press, 1959). He restated it in a generalized form in "The Evolving Form and Organization of the Metropolis," in *Issues in Urban Economics,* ed. Harvey Perloff and Lowdon Wingo, Jr. (Baltimore: The Johns Hopkins Press, 1968).

The theory begins with the assumption that, other things being equal, both households and businesses will locate so as to maximize accessibility to other people and activities with whom they have, or need to have, frequent contacts. Households will try to locate within easy commuting reach of the present jobs of wage-earning members of the household, and within easy reach of potential alternative employment opportunities. They will also be concerned with access to shopping, schools, cultural and recreational activities, and friends and relatives, but the link between home and job is likely to be the most important one, if only because the journey to and from work is repeated so many times. For businesses, accessibility is a more complicated concept. Ideally, any business firm wants easy access to a large pool of potential employees, to raw materials and other inputs to the productive process, to other firms with which it has frequent intercourse (as suppliers of services and market information), and to its customers. Because it is usually impossible to have good access to all of these simultaneously, firms settle for good access to those people and activities that are most important for their particular line of business. Thus, financial firms that depend heavily on close contact with other firms for information and business deals tend to cluster together in central locations and worry little about access to raw materials; heavy-manufacturing enterprises tend to seek more isolated locations that provide good access to raw materials and easy shipping of finished products; and retailers seek locations that maximize their access to customers.

Inaccessibility is overcome by transportation, but transportation costs both money and time. Thus, the simpler models of the theory measure access in terms of transport costs: maximizing accessibility is a matter of minimizing transport costs. Like all theoretical constructs, this is an oversimplification.

Small differences in transport costs may make little difference, and factors like comfort, convenience, and reliability are often more important than costs pure and simple. Nonetheless, it is reasonable to say, as a first approximation, that locators are concerned with minimizing transport costs.

The second assumption of the theory is that, other things being equal once again, households and businesses will try to maximize the quality and quantity of the buildings and sites they occupy. That is, people will prefer more spacious and higher-quality housing to poorer housing. They will prefer locations in good neighborhoods, with congenial neighbors, attractive physical surroundings, conveniences like easy parking and good schools, and other public services. Similarly, business firms will prefer locations where they can build, buy, or rent quarters that are especially well suited to the specific nature of their operations. This may be a high-rise building for the headquarters of a national corporation, a ground-floor location on a busy street for a specialty shop, or a sprawling one-story plant for a large manufacturing operation. The danger of oversimplification here, as in the theory of household location, lies in defining this complex of factors as the demand for space, assuming that more spacious housing also means better neighborhood amenities and better public services. This is often, but not always, the case.

The theory's third assumption is that locators seek to minimize the cost of the quarters they occupy, while simultaneously seeking to maximize their quality. Households and firms alike are subject to a budget constraint. Funds are limited, and more money spent for housing or for business premises means that less is available for all the other things that people consume.

Obviously, it is not possible to maximize accessibility (or, as the theory usually puts it, to minimize transport costs),

maximize quality or spaciousness, and at the same time minimize costs. Households and firms must trade off among access,
space, and price so as to achieve that combination of results
which is most nearly optimal for each of them.[2] In general,
accessibility is greatest in the central parts of metropolitan
areas, where people have the greatest range of job and shopping opportunities, and businesses have access to the largest
pool of potential employees, customers, and other business
firms. But this very concentration—this density—means that
spaciousness tends to be very limited in, and near, central
areas; the maximum in spaciousness tends to be found on the
periphery of metropolitan areas, where access is least. So most
locators must trade off access against space, the individual
decision depending upon the relative intensity of the desire or
need for accessibility compared to the desire or need for
spaciousness.[3] Also, the prices of land and buildings tend to
be higher in locations with very good accessibility and/or with
good neighborhood amenities and public services. Thus, location decisions also require trading off access or spaciousness
against price, the individual decision depending upon the relative intensity of the desire or need for access or space compared to the desire or need for objects of expenditure other
than housing or business premises.

---

2. The reader familiar with elementary microeconomic theory will recognize
   this as a three-dimensional indifference map problem, in which the household or firm tries to find that combination of three "commodities"—access,
   space, and all other goods and services—that places it at the highest level
   of utility or output.
3. Note the qualified way in which this argument is put. Some locators are
   indeed able to combine a lot of access with a lot of space—for example,
   people employed in plants or offices located in the outer parts of metropolitan areas. As activity becomes more decentralized, more such cases arise.
   But even here there is some trade-off: at the periphery of the metropolitan
   area, access to other things—like cultural attractions and jobs other than
   the one now held—is likely to be poor.

It should be clear that the outcome of the trade-off process depends heavily upon income and wealth. At one extreme, the very richest households and firms can disregard cost and, at a very high price, combine a great deal of accessibility with a great deal of spaciousness. The $1 million-plus town house on Manhattan's East Side or the $500,000 cooperative apartment in Watergate in Washington is highly accessible, spacious, and comfortable, with good neighborhood amenities. At the other extreme, low-income households must sacrifice quality, and sometimes a good deal of accessibility as well, in order to find any housing at all within their budget constraints. However, the great majority of location decisions are made by locators who fall between these extremes of wealth and who both must, and can, make marginal, not polar, choices among access, space, and price, sacrificing a moderate amount of one desirable attribute for a moderately larger amount of another.

The trade-off theory by itself does not predict just what the pattern of intrametropolitan location will be. Additional theorizing is necessary to spell out the process through which the trade-offs work themselves out in the economic environment of modern cities and to explain some of the striking regularities in urban spatial structure that can be seen in most large urban areas in North America and Western Europe. One theory about the process itself is found in the "bid-rent" model originally developed by William Alonso.[4] Each household or business firm is assumed to be willing to pay a higher price or rent for those locations that have the most accessibility (for that type of activity) than for locations with lesser accessibility, but how much more (that is the bid-rent) depends upon how highly other attributes—those we have gathered together

---

4. See William Alonso, *Location and Land Use* (Cambridge, Mass.: Harvard University Press, 1964).

under the umbrella term, *spaciousness*—are valued relative to access. For example, one would expect that households headed by wage earners with limited skills and earning potential would value access highly, because they would be concerned greatly about being near the largest possible pool of alternative job opportunities. In this way they can readily learn about employment opportunities and will not be stranded by the instability of employment that characterizes low-skill occupational groups. Also, they would be greatly concerned about minimizing transport costs, because such costs can be a high fraction of their low earnings.

In contrast, wage earners with higher skills and earning potential can be less concerned about the money costs of commuting and are more secure about the stability of their present job and their ability to find a better one from the much wider array of opportunities for which they are qualified. Thus, the low-skill household would have a sharp preference for accessibility, and its bid-rent would decline sharply as accessibility falls off, while the high-skill household would have a much milder preference for access, and its bid-rent would decline only slightly with declines in accessibility. Similar considerations apply to different types of business. The central office of a large corporation would have a steeper bid-rent curve than, say, a data-processing center, because the latter can have good accessibility by telephone and does not need physical proximity to other activities.

In any given part of the urban area, those activities whose bid-rents are highest for those locations will predominate by bidding away sites from activities for which those locations are less valuable. This is shown in Figure 1-1.[5] The broken

---

5. For this graphic adaptation of the Alonso model, I am indebted to Edwin Mills, whose *Urban Economics* (Chicago: Scott, Foresman, 1972) presents it in connection with an elegant discussion of the theory of urban structure (Chap. 4, p. 75).

lines are the bid-rent curves for four different groups; the heavy solid line is a curve composed of the segments that have the highest bids at those locations. Central office activities (AA′) will dominate at the very center of the area, because access is worth more for such activities than for any others.

FIGURE 1-1 *The Location of Activities in Urban Areas*

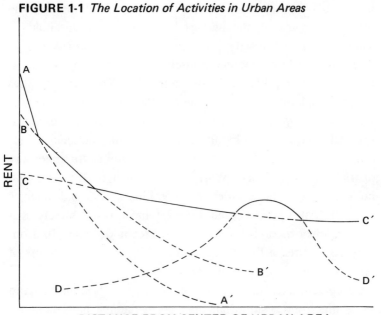

A A′: Central office activities
B B′: Housing demand, low- and moderate-income households
C C′: Housing demand, middle- and upper-income households
D D′: Large-scale manufacturing activities

Low- and moderate-income housing (BB′) will predominate just beyond the very center, while middle- and upper-income housing (CC′) will predominate in much of the rest of the urban area, for the reasons explained in the preceding paragraph. Large-scale manufacturing (DD′) will predominate at some outlying locations on the assumption that road transport costs for shipment of products and receipt of materials are lower in suburban locations.

This helps to explain why low-income households tend to locate in inner-city areas, despite the fact that land values are relatively high in such locations and, indeed, to explain how such households manage to bid *any* locations away from higher-income families. The explanation is that the demand for spaciousness on the part of higher-income households is such that the inner-city locations are simply worth less to them than to lower-income households. All this, of course, is a gross oversimplification, for preferences and opportunities differ considerably, even among families with similar income levels. In every large city, there are upper-income households that value access very highly and, as a result, succeed in bidding away sites from the poor. In fact, there are inner-city districts in New York, Washington, Chicago, London, and numerous other large cities that combine access and amenity so well that upper-income families have progressively displaced lower-income households in recent decades. In London, opponents of this process refer to it as "gentrification" of previously working-class districts.

More generally, middle- and upper-income households tend to be much more suburban than lower-income households in North America, Britain, Germany, and, to an increasing extent, other European countries. There is an additional theoretical explanation for this, one that is independent of the accessibility arguments developed above. It is probably true that the cost of commuting—in money, time, and all-around disagreeableness—is proportionate to earnings, because the rich can afford to value their preferences for leisure and comfort more than the poor. Thus, so long as high-income households have the more intense demand for better housing quality, spaciousness, and the like that the empirical evidence suggests they do, high-income households will tend to live further out, where spaciousness can be achieved more cheaply.[6]

Virtually all the theories of urban structure assume, and are consistent with, the observed fact that land values and the density of land use in an urban area are very high at the center, decline very sharply as one moves away from the center, and flatten out just a few miles beyond the center. It is self-evident why land values and density should be very high at the center, despite the decentralization of economic activity. The centers of the larger cities remain their points of maximum accessibility, and maximum accessibility is of real importance to a very rapidly growing sector of the modern economy, the provision of professional, managerial, financial, and governmental services usually carried out in office buildings.

But it is not self-evident why the decline in land values and density should be so steep and then flatten out.[7] If accessibility is the key, and minimizing transport costs the goal, land values and density should fall off smoothly and proportionately throughout the urban area, as long as transport costs are proportional to distance, which they generally are. The theoretical reason for the shape of the land-value gradient is a simple one: it is possible and profitable to capture the advantages of central area accessibility, for those activities for which it is important, by building more intensively in the central areas, that is, by applying more capital to land in the form of taller buildings and greater site coverage. As long as this is possible, much higher prices can be paid for central business district land than for land just beyond it, which may have no loca-

---

6. This theoretical proposition was first proved algebraically by Richard Muth in *Cities and Housing* (Chicago: University of Chicago Press, 1969), pp. 29 ff.
7. That is, why the rent or density function should be nonlinear rather than linear.

tional attractions at all as sites for offices, luxury housing, and the like.

This brief review of the theory of urban economic structure was not designed to provide definitive and comprehensive explanations of why cities are shaped the way they are, but rather to indicate that urban economists do have a theoretical context, incomplete and inadequate though it may be, in which urban economic problems can be studied. Urban form is not the result of random and accidental historical developments that, strangely enough, have produced very similar outcomes in most large cities, but rather seems to be the result of the working out of comprehensible economic factors. Accidents do occur (for example, the location of the nation's capital in Washington rather than in New York or Philadelphia); the specific geography of a city is important (for example, the fact that Manhattan is an island or that Chicago is a semi-circular city without hills); and government intervention in the city-building process, through zoning, transportation investments, reservation of space for parks, and many other actions can be crucial. Nonetheless, the economic forces are strong enough to have produced cities with very similar spatial structures, despite differences in history, geography, and many other factors.

Some Important Economic Concepts

The central analytical issue in urban economics is, as we have just seen, the spatial distribution of activities. In grappling with this analytical issue and its implications for urban problems and policies, the economist naturally draws upon a whole range of conceptual tools peculiar to the "dismal science." And a dismal science it is, for economics is essentially no more than the study of the costs and benefits of choices among alternatives, saying again and again that societies and individuals face hard choices and that there are few opportunities that have no costs.

The economist's measure of costs is "opportunity costs." Any particular course of action that involves the use of resources can be said to have an opportunity cost in the sense that the same resources might have been employed in other uses, and those other uses would have produced some public or private benefits. The opportunity costs of the actual course of action chosen, therefore, are equal to the benefits foregone by the loss of the opportunity to use the resources in other ways. In cities, the benefits foregone by using a particular piece of land in one way—say, for a parking lot—rather than another—say, for a high-rise building—are often the most important of all the costs associated with economic decision making.

A corollary to the opportunity-cost concept is the concept of "sunk costs." Opportunity costs refer only to the costs of resources that otherwise might be employed to provide different kinds of goods or services. They do *not* refer to costs incurred in the past, because we cannot reuse for other purposes resources consumed at some earlier time. The labor devoted to use A last year is not available for use B this year; the materials consumed in building a battleship in World War II are not available, without expensive salvage work, for building schools now. These are sunk costs, and to economists they are no costs at all.

Thus, economic reasoning suggests that frequently there is little cost to more intensive use of already constructed facilities, and that such use should not be restricted as a by-product of an effort to recoup costs incurred in the past. For example, if an existing bridge has substantial unused capacity, there would be little or no cost occasioned were additional cars to use the bridge. Tolls are typically imposed to recover previously incurred costs, rather than current resource costs. But tolls usually will discourage use of the bridge to some extent at least, a fact that makes no sense at all in economic terms if there is indeed spare capacity on the bridge.

On the other hand, the sunk-costs concept on occasion suggests the abandonment of already constructed facilities that are still physically serviceable, but are in the wrong place or otherwise impose high current costs. The original costs of the facilities are no longer relevant to decision making. For example, because of population shifts, cities sometimes find themselves with serviceable school buildings in areas with few school-age children. Such buildings may be usable only by spending a great deal to bus the children to school—a current cost. To do this might amount to throwing good money after bad.

Another set of crucial economic concepts concerns the relative intensity of demand for particular goods, services, or attributes. The economist's term is "elasticity" of demand, and this is measured in terms of both the price of the good and the income of those who demand it. Demand is said to be relatively elastic with respect to price if a small increase in its price will result in a sharp falloff in the quantity sought by buyers (and vice versa). It is said to be inelastic if a price change results in a less than proportionate change in the quantity sought. Observed price elasticities for a particular good are a consequence of purchasers' trade-offs among all the goods and services they seek to buy. Thus, to return to our analysis of urban spatial structure, the curves in Figure 1-1 imply that middle- and upper-income households would not buy a great deal more accessibility if its price were reduced, but would buy a lot more housing (or spaciousness) if *its* price were reduced. Their demand for space is a lot more elastic (or sensitive to price) than their demand for access.

Information about price elasticities is important for a wide range of urban problems. It is crucial to know how the demand for housing will respond to policy measures that raise or lower the price of housing, such as subsidy programs for new housing aimed at low- and moderate-income families. It is similarly important to know how changes in transit fares or bridge tolls will affect the use of those facilities.

The elasticity of demand with respect to income—how rapidly or slowly demand increases as income rises—is also vital information for economic reasoning. Figure 1-1 suggests that the demand for accessibility barely rises, and may even fall, as income rises, whereas the reverse is true of the demand for space. As we will see in connection with the discussion of housing policies later in this book, the income elasticity of demand for housing plays a crucial role in the choice among alternative housing policies: if income elasticity is very considerable, then the best way of providing better housing for the poor may simply be to increase their incomes.

Whether this will be the best policy depends also upon another type of elasticity—the elasticity of supply with respect to price, that is, how much more of a commodity is offered by suppliers in response to a small increase in price. In the case of housing, if supply is inelastic—that is, if a rise in price resulting from the increased demand that will result if the incomes of the poor are increased produces only a very small expansion of the stock of housing—then the policy will not do very much to improve the housing conditions of the poor. The calculation or estimation of elasticities of price, income, demand, or supply is not easy with respect to most urban public policy concerns, but a great deal of empirical work has been done on the subject.

Yet another set of economic concepts important for the urban economy and its problems relates to how costs change as the size or scale of activities increase, that is, the nature of economies of scale. The existence of positive economies of scale is the essential reason why cities develop to begin with. The very rapid growth of cities after the onset of the industrial revolution is largely explained by the fact that the new technology called for production in large plants in which the costs of a unit of output were much lower than in the earlier small-scale cottage and handicraft industry. Cities grew up around one or a few large plants, simply because those plants employed so many people. Cities also grew as trade centers and continue to grow in "post-industrial" societies, because of scale economies of another type—the necessity of having large markets to support, at feasible costs, the provision of a wide range of goods and services, including those provided by governments and nonprofit organizations. Only in large urban areas are enough customers concentrated to justify (except at extremely high unit costs) full-line department stores, a wide range of specialty shops, museums, symphony orchestras, teaching hospitals, and many other such services.

As cities grow, a phenomenon closely related to scale economies appears—"agglomeration economies." These are the advantages to each firm or household that stem from the presence nearby of many similar firms and households, with complementary needs and labor supplies, offsetting fluctuations in sales, output, and purchases, and the personal interaction that fosters innovation. In theory, there is some scale at which each type of scale economy or agglomeration economy should be exhausted—that is, unit costs should start to rise. *Diseconomies* of scale are then said to be present. The widespread belief that the very largest urban areas are now too big and that efforts to limit (or reverse) their further growth should be made rests on the allegation that scale diseconomies, like congestion, pollution, high costs of public services, and so forth, now exceed the scale economies. Clearly, the extent to which this allegation is valid has a bearing on every aspect of urban public policy.

A fair amount of economic reasoning is devoted to piercing what has been called "the veil of money," that is, to distinguishing between money costs and "real," or resource, costs. Economists typically try hard to measure things in money terms, because quantification is not very useful unless there is a common denominator, which money is. But economics tries not to let the measuring rod blind it to the underlying reality. Money really does not matter, except as a device to facilitate transactions (and measurement); what does matter is the use of human and material resources. Thus, opportunity costs and sunk costs refer to resource costs, rather than to financial outlays.

For example, consider the use of parkland for purposes other than parks—for roads or public buildings—a not uncommon source of controversy in American urban areas where land is relatively scarce and therefore expensive. Using parkland for other uses is often attractive to public agencies because there is no dollar cost involved in acquisition of the land. However, there may be very large opportunity costs if recreational land is highly valued by the community, as it usually is in urban areas. When the parkland is taken for other uses, the costs take the form of the recreational benefits foregone.

Another major concern of economists is with the dimension of time. The fact of mortality—the shortness of life—makes most of us prefer benefits enjoyed now to benefits realized at a later date and also makes most of us prefer to defer costs to later periods. This "time preference" gives rise to the financial phenomenon called interest, which is the price paid to induce holders of money to defer their use of the money to command resources to a later date. But there is a real (resource) consequence as well. Other things being equal (as they so seldom are in reality), solutions to problems that can take effect soon are better than those that take years to show results. There is good reason, that is, aside from skepticism, to shun "pie in the sky bye and bye" and to demand quick results. For example, additional years of schooling tend to improve future income-earning prospects, but the results occur over periods of many years—a person's working lifetime. When the long payoff period is taken into account (by using a rate of interest to discount the deferred benefits), increased expenditure for education is likely to prove a much less effective means of reducing poverty than immediate direct cash grants to the poor.

There is another aspect of the concern with time. The use of resources has a time dimension, and resources underutilized this year are simply wasted for the most part. This is especially true of human resources. Labor services that are not used at all or used below their productive capabilities in one time period are gone forever. Thus, both the time dimension and the distinction between real and money costs suggest strongly that ways should be found to utilize unemployed people in worthwhile jobs for which they may be qualified, such as aides in schools and hospitals and as maintenance and custodial workers in connection with public services of all kinds. The jobs to be done and the people available to do the jobs should not be separated by the barrier of the immediate dollar costs. There is a converse to this. Postponement of a project does not merely postpone the realization of benefits and the incurrence of money costs; it also postpones real costs, because during the delay, the resources are available for other uses.

Yet another basic economic concept of major importance in urban economic prescription is that of "external costs and benefits." In competitive markets, transactions between buyers and sellers are based on their respective perception of costs and benefits to *them,* that is, internal costs and benefits. Most transactions have some effects on third parties. For example, if one builds an architecturally distinguished house, his neighbors are benefited; if one builds a singularly ugly house, his neighbors suffer. In very many cases, the costs and benefits external to the participants in a transaction are rather minor ones, and so we ignore them. In other cases, we seek to limit these externalities by law—for example, by requiring air-pollution control devices on motor vehicles and in industrial plants.

As a society becomes more complex and interdependent, and as people live more closely together, which is what happens with increasing urbanization, the likelihood that significant externalities will arise increases sharply. We are growing increasingly concerned about the external effects of individuals' decisions on waste disposal, or on land use, or on modes of transportation, or about the lack of educational attainment by some children.

A major concern, then, is with means for minimizing the external costs and maximizing the potential external benefits from decisions made by individuals. But even in an urban society, not all decisions give rise to really important externalities. In a society that prizes freedom of choice and action by individuals, groups, and local governments, it is important to pinpoint those decisions that do not involve major externalities, decisions that can be freely made on the basis of internal costs and benefits. Such freedom has the major economic advantage of being consistent with a more efficient allocation of resources.

Efficiency and Equity in Economics

But what is an "efficient allocation of resources"? Any answer to this question must be founded on a very basic value judgment concerning the point of view that is crucial in appraising economic performance—who decides what is best? The great majority of Western economists share a common value judgment about this: we believe that, despite ignorance, mistakes, and ineptitude, on balance each person can appraise his own well-being better than can anyone else. Once that is accepted, it follows that the ideal allocation of resources is that which maximizes the well-being, or welfare, of all the individuals in a society, as judged by those individuals.

However, because each individual is appraising his own welfare, we cannot possibly know whether an action or event that reduces one person's welfare in order to enhance another's is really improving the sum total of well-being in a society. Economists employ a rigorous definition of efficiency in the allocation of resources that avoids any pretensions that we can know the unknowable. This definition was developed by Vilfredo Pareto, mentioned earlier in this chapter as the inventor of a generalized description of the distribution of incomes that also seems to describe the size distribution of cities. Pareto's truly monumental contribution to economic reasoning was his definition of the conditions for economic efficiency and optimal performance of an economy.

Given available resources and technology, Pareto efficiency is achieved when no change in resource allocation—no change in the combination of land, labor, and capital used in production, no change in the mix of goods and services produced, no change in the mix of goods and services each household consumes—can improve the well-being of some persons without worsening that of others. The conditions that must prevail in order for this to be achieved are complex and require simultaneous resolution of a huge number of production and consumption decisions. The Pareto model is one of great elegance, even beauty, but this is not the place to develop it.[8]

The mechanism for achieving Pareto efficiency is the price system operating through perfectly competitive markets. This assures that prices will equal the marginal cost of production; that returns to the factors of production will be proportional to their marginal contributions to production; that the different factors of production will be combined to produce different goods and services so that the ratio of their marginal product is the same for all commodities, and all consumers' willingness to substitute an increment of one commodity for a marginal decrease in another will be equated.

Perfect competition is by no means the rule in a modern economy. Pareto efficiency cannot be fully achieved where there are important monopoly elements, when producers or consumers are less than fully informed about the possibilities for bettering their positions, or when there are significant external economies and diseconomies. Still more important, roughly one-third of our gross national product (GNP) is based not on market decisions and the price system, but on collective decisions made by government; a significant portion of the two-thirds of GNP produced by the private sector is heavily affected by government decisions and actions. The "impossibility theorem" for which Professor Kenneth Arrow was awarded the Nobel Prize in economic science shows that it is not possible to achieve the conditions for Pareto efficiency in collective decision making.

We need not despair, however. It is possible to reduce the

---

8. For an educated person to go through life without having been exposed to the experience of comprehending the Pareto scheme is an intellectual loss on a par with being unfamiliar with the Copernican revolution, Machiavelli, the discovery of DNA, or the theory of the expanding universe.

influence of monopoly elements in the economy; moreover, some of the worst urban problems, like congestion, pollution, poverty, and bad housing, simply do *not* result from monopoly power at all. Similarly, it is possible to improve substantially the information on which decisions are based; this is being done constantly in our economy. Also, public policy can be directed at "internalizing" external economies, for example, by forcing polluters to bear the costs their environmental damage imposes on others. Finally, even in the public sector, there are important opportunities for simulating the market decision making that would lead toward Pareto efficiency, by using indirect means for estimating the nature and quantity of public goods people would demand if they were provided through competitive markets and then supplying that mix of public goods. Such estimation has been done, for example, in connection with the demand for outdoor recreational opportunities. To be sure, none of this will bring us to pure Pareto efficiency; but the "second-best" solutions that are necessary can be truly second, rather than tenth, best, if Pareto efficiency remains a goal toward which economic performance aspires.

Even a Pareto-efficient economy need not be a Pareto-optimal economy. Optimality, in the Pareto scheme, also requires that the distribution of income and wealth be equitable. Economists can and do measure the distribution of income and wealth and the effects of proposed actions on this distribution, but they can say little as economists to define what is equitable. It must be the society as a whole that defines equity, for it is too important to leave to the experts. Indeed, debate about the proper distribution of income and wealth is a persistent, central issue in the politics of all democratic countries, and a consensus must be reached if democracy is to survive. It should be said, however, that nearly all economists—like most other people—agree that the distribution of income and wealth that would be produced by a Pareto-efficient market economy, without government intervention, is far too unequal to be acceptable, and that some equalizing action by government is essential.

This book applies the tools of economic reasoning to the major problems evident in American urban areas. It examines what economists can and do say about the economic aspects of these problems and about the economic aspects of policies appropriate to the resolution of the problems. The focus is on problems and policies, largely public policies, rather than on the analytic tools now utilized in urban economics. However, the analytic tools and concepts explored briefly in this chapter provide the basis for the choice of problems that are dealt with.

First, only those urban problems that are substantially affected by the spatial distribution of activities in urban areas are included in this book. Thus, the book discusses urban poverty, for poverty in its urban form is distinguished by marked geographic concentration. It covers housing, land use, and transportation, subjects for which spatial structure is of the essence. But it does not deal with health problems and policies, for example, because those problems seem bound up with the economics and organization of the health care "industry," with the spatial dimensions a minor issue.

Second, an important emphasis is on distinguishing between efficiency and equity, that is, resource misallocation and income inequality, as a source of urban difficulties, and between the efficiency and equity consequences of proposed solutions. The problems selected for study are rich with opportunities for making such distinctions—for example, the extent to which poverty is "structurally" related to the decentralization of

economic activity and thus curable by resource allocation
changes, rather than by income redistribution pure and simple,
or the extent to which bad housing is a consequence of low
income rather than resource misallocation.

Third, the problems selected are closely interrelated. We
begin with a discussion of poverty and move on to housing as
the next step, because of the connection just noted between
bad housing and low incomes. Housing is far and away the
most important land use in cities, and thus there is need for an
explicit discussion of land use policies. Land use, in turn, is,
in cities, a major determinant of environmental problems and
is both a determinant and consequence of transportation needs
and services. Finally, we deal with the problem of paying for
those solutions that must be handled by government action,
and paying in ways that do not aggravate spatial maldistribution or otherwise move away from Pareto efficiency and do
not conflict with common notions of equity. These are surely
some of the most important urban problems about which
economists have something useful to say.

2

The Problems:
An Overview

For close to a decade, cataloging the ills of America's urban areas has been something of a national sport in which anyone can play—presidential commissions, journalists, academic experts, and the man in the street as well. Any list of problems is likely to be dominated by the difficulties of the large central cities of the country's metropolitan areas, for these are the places that have experienced open revolt, despair, or both. But there is another set of problems that affects both cities and their surrounding suburbs and relates to the effects of the growing size of urban concentrations on the quality of life in America. This is the seeming inability of our wealth to buy an environment in which everyday living is convenient, abrasion-free, visually satisfying, not prone to breakdown, and free from a built-in ecological self-destruct mechanism.

Economists have no special expertise regarding some of the many problems. In this chapter, an effort is made to say something about the nature and dimensions of seven major problems, each of which has important economic causes or consequences. In subsequent chapters, each of the problems is discussed more exhaustively in conjunction with an analysis of

31

alternative ways of solving the problems. It is difficult to really understand the nature of the difficulties we confront without trying to think about how we should go about overcoming the difficulties. This is especially true because the seven problems listed in this chapter are not wholly separate ones. They interact with one another, and a possible solution for one set of difficulties may help solve another set or may aggravate other problems.

The problems this book focuses on are the following:

1. Increasing proportions of the populations of the central cities, especially in the North and East, are made up of blacks or Spanish-speaking minority groups whose economic and social situation is decidedly worse than that of white Anglo-America. A significant percentage of these urban minorities is poor, however poverty is defined. Indeed, aside from the elderly, poverty in large cities is to a considerable extent a racial or ethnic phenomenon.

2. In the older cities, again mostly in the North and East, the stock of what can be called "social capital"—housing and public and institutional facilities—is in bad shape. There is a good deal of physical decay and deterioration. There is even more functional obsolescence in that many facilities are suited in design, capacity, location, and public acceptability to the first quarter of the twentieth century rather than to its last quarter. This partly reflects the concentrations of poor people in the older cities; it partly is simply a result of age; but it also reflects an array of obstacles to adjustment to changing times.

3. There is a more general set of housing problems. Urban areas have populations with varied housing preferences and varied abilities to pay for housing; they have a slowly growing and changing supply of housing that often does not match preferences and incomes very well. This is especially so for

the poor and for lower-middle-income groups. But for others
as well there is growing dissatisfaction with the range of choice
offered, choice among locations, housing types, and neighborhood characteristics.

4. The distribution of economic activity within urban areas
has been changing rapidly in the past two decades. The dominant trend has been the decentralization of most kinds of
economic activity away from central cities, which has powerful effects on job opportunities, tax bases, and transportation,
and which has dramatically changed land-use patterns in the
newer areas.

5. Growth in population and economic activity clearly is
associated with serious ecological hazards in the form of air
and water pollution, and pollution tends to be worse in densely
populated places than in sparsely settled areas. It is generally
believed that urban growth itself has led to a more general
deterioration in the character of the urban environment, pollution aside—less access to natural open space and recreational
opportunity; higher levels of noise and congestion; less of a
sense of cleanliness, lack of clutter, visual beauty.

6. There is almost complete dissatisfaction with transportation facilities and services in the larger urban areas, despite
the expenditure of billions of dollars of public funds in the last
decade to improve urban transportation. The major difficulties
include access to downtowns for both people and goods, especially at peak hours; movement within and among the older
suburban areas; travel to recreational facilities; and movement
between nearby urban areas, especially along the North Atlan-
tic seaboard, the "megalopolis."

7. There is no scarcity of "solutions" to these problems,
but almost all solutions require more resources and the money
to command these resources. But there have been immense
difficulties in financing governmental action. State and local

governments have been increasing their taxes rapidly, in the face of real voter resistance; but despite this, the large cities feel that they are on the verge of bankruptcy. Both suburban and central city governments find themselves far from providing the levels of service the problems seem to demand.

Race and Poverty in the Cities[1]

The size and composition of the urban population depends upon natural factors—birth and death rates—and upon millions of individual decisions about the choice of residential location. Since the end of large-scale European immigration at the time of World War I, there have been four great streams of internal migration within the United States. First, there has been the westward movement from the older sections of the country to the West Coast and Southwest in pursuit of economic opportunity and the sun. Second, rural and small-town white Americans have been migrating in large numbers to the metropolitan areas at a rate averaging 200,000 a year since 1950.

Third, within the metropolitan areas, whites have been moving from the central cities to the suburbs, also in large numbers. Since 1950, net migration from the central cities has averaged more than 500,000 a year, and this has been heavily concentrated in the large older cities in the North and Midwest. Their places have been taken by those in the fourth stream of migration, that is, blacks migrating from the rural

---

1. A brilliant and comprehensive discussion of the facts and the consequences can be found in the *Report* of the National Advisory Commission on Civil Disorders (the Kerner Commission), which was appointed by the president in July 1967 and reported in February 1968; see especially Chapters 6–9. Of course, the data used in this section draw on the 1970 census and other more recent sources.

South to the larger cities, to some extent in the South, but more often in the North and West. When combined, these streams have produced what we see today: a heavily urbanized population, more than half in suburbs that are virtually all white and the rest in central cities that are increasingly black.

It is worth looking more closely at the changes in the black (or nonwhite) population.[2] In 1950, there were 15 million American Negroes; 10 million lived in the South, over half of them in rural areas. By 1970, the black population was 22.7 million; 12.1 million lived in the South and 10.6 million elsewhere, more than double the number in 1950. In 1950, 43 percent of all Negroes lived in central cities. By 1970, 58 percent of all blacks were central-city residents. In contrast, only 28 percent of all whites lived in the central cities in 1970, compared to 34 percent in 1950. If these trends are projected ahead to 1985,[3] well over 60 percent of all nonwhites will be central-city residents; the nonwhite population of northern and western cities will be at least 7 million greater than in 1970, while the white population will be 2 million (or more) fewer.

---

2. In this book, the terms "Negro" or "black" and "nonwhite" are used almost as if they were interchangeable. Although Negroes comprise almost 90 percent of the nonwhite population, there are some significant differences. In 1970, there were 2.9 million persons of races other than white or black in the United States—roughly one-fourth of them American Indians and the remainder persons of Asian and Pacific Island descent and Eskimos. Many Indians are desperately poor, but few live in urban areas. Most other nonwhites do live in urban areas (about half in Hawaii and California), but relatively few are poor. Thus, the major *urban* problems associated with race and poverty are, in fact, very largely afflictions of blacks and not of other nonwhites. The large minority groups that live in cities and have difficulties similar to those of blacks are those of Spanish-American descent, but these are largely classified as "white" in Census statistics.

3. As they were in a study prepared for the National Commission on Urban Problems (June 1968).

These movements have had a striking impact on the racial composition of cities. In 1950, a little over 10 percent of the population of metropolitan central cities and a similar share of the small-town and rural population were black, but only about 5 percent of the suburban population. Since then, the suburbs have changed little in racial composition, and the small towns and rural areas have become more white. But the Negro percentage of the central-city population has risen sharply, to just over 20 percent in 1971. If present trends continue, the central cities will be 30 percent Negro by 1985. This change has not been uniform among central cities. The smaller ones (with populations of less than 250,000) are by and large no more black than they were in 1950, but the Negro percentage in the central cities of the larger metropolitan areas has more than doubled. The central cities of the twelve largest metropolitan areas now contain nearly two-thirds of the black population outside the South and nearly one-third of the Negro total in the United States.

White immigrants, in an earlier era, also concentrated within the central cities, where there was cheap housing and where their friends and relatives lived. As the immigrants' incomes rose and as they themselves were "Americanized," the ethnic concentrations broke up, in moves to other neighborhoods and to suburbs. As a result, as the Kerner Commission pointed out, "most middle-class neighborhoods—both in the suburbs and within central cities—have no distinctive ethnic character, except that they are white." But the expansion of the urban black population has not followed this pattern of dispersal. Despite increases in incomes, most black families have been contained, by one discriminatory device or another, within predominantly black neighborhoods. The statistical evidence indicates that the extent of residential segregation in the largest cities changed little from 1940 to 1950 and from 1950 to 1960 and that it has actually increased since 1960.

The racial ghetto problem also affects two other minority groups. Since 1950, there has been a large-scale migration of Puerto Ricans to northeastern cities, especially New York, where more than 1.2 million Puerto Ricans and Hispanic immigrants from elsewhere in Latin America now live. The large Mexican-American population of the Southwest, mostly in California and Texas, has been increasingly concentrating in cities in that region. As with blacks, the urban Spanish-American populations will continue to increase rapidly, even if migration stops, because they are youthful populations with high birthrates. Like Negroes, they find it difficult to break out of ghettos, because of poverty, discrimination, and cultural isolation (particularly the language barrier). Whatever the reasons, in New York, Los Angeles, San Diego, and San Antonio, to name only the largest cities, the dimensions of the ghetto problem are much greater than the classification "percent Negro" alone would suggest.

Racial ghettos would be obnoxious in any event, but they are clearly associated with poverty. The Social Security Administration defines the "poverty line" as an annual income, based on family size and geographic location, below which households are considered to be poor (in 1971, the poverty line was roughly $4,100 for an urban family of four). Only about 10 percent of white central-city residents have incomes below this poverty line, and 20 percent of these are elderly people. But nearly 30 percent of black central-city residents live in poverty, and all but a few of these are younger families. Indeed, the most striking aspect of racial poverty in the cities is how much it affects children. Although only one-fourth of the children under age eighteen in cities are black, poor black children outnumber poor white children; well over one-third of all black children under age eighteen live in poor families. The great majority of black families headed by a female with children under age six live in poverty; there are over 200,000 such families in central cities.

The Spanish-American minority groups add substantially to the scope of the urban poverty problem. Close to one-third of Puerto Rican population falls below the officially defined poverty line, and Mexican-Americans are only slightly better off. In both cases, 60 percent of households headed by females are below the poverty line. In New York, average Puerto Rican incomes are even below the low averages for blacks; in the Southwest, Mexican-Americans do somewhat better than blacks on the average, but even so they have incomes only 75 percent as high as white "Anglos."

All told, the racial aspects of the urban poverty problem are striking. In 1971, there were 8.9 million people in central cities whose incomes were below the poverty line. Of these about 1.3 million were 65 and over; 4.5 million were younger Negroes, Puerto Ricans and Mexican-Americans; and 3.1 million were white "Anglos" under 65. The numbers in the first and last group have been declining steadily; the numbers in the middle group have been declining very slowly indeed.

Racial poverty is in part a consequence of family structure and age composition of the population. A very large percentage of urban blacks and Puerto Ricans are young children and their mothers, who are effectively outside the labor force and thus dependent on the earnings of others (or outside assistance) for their support. But minority-group members of the labor force have lower skills and training than whites and are discriminated against in job placement and promotion; therefore, they earn much less, to support their larger and younger families. Even more important, they find it much more difficult to get, and hold, secure, full-time jobs.

The spring of 1968 was a period of high prosperity in the United States, but unemployment remained high among urban nonwhites. For adults, the nonwhite unemployment was 6 percent, and for teen-agers (age sixteen to nineteen), more than 25 percent, about double the rates for the same groups of urban whites. In addition to the 350,000 unemployed nonwhites, there were over 700,000 "underemployed"—persons who had dropped out of the competition for jobs in despair or who held part-time, insecure, low-wage jobs. Thus, for the 8 million central-city nonwhites of working age (age sixteen to sixty-four), there was a "deficit" of over a million jobs.

Residential segregation and unemployment reinforce each other. Even without discrimination, unemployed families would not be able to afford to move to more expensive housing outside the ghettos. On the other hand, ghetto residents find it difficult indeed to participate in expanding employment opportunities in suburban locations, because transportation is difficult and costly and because they simply do not know of the job vacancies in distant places. It has been estimated that, as of the mid-1950s, over 30,000 jobs had been lost to the black communities in Chicago and Detroit because of housing segregation.[4]

It can be argued persuasively that discrimination, housing conditions, poverty, and the consequent indicators of social malaise were even worse for the nineteenth- and early twentieth-century immigrants than they are for urban blacks and Spanish-speaking Americans today. The early immigrant minority groups overcame their difficulties often with little external assistance. Why cannot today's immigrants to the cities do so as well? Why is there so much demand for purposeful

---

4. See John F. Kain, "Housing Segregation, Negro Employment and Metropolitan Decentralization," *Quarterly Journal of Economics,* May 1968.

public action? The answers are a mixture of social and economic reasons. Discrimination on the basis of color is easier to effect and, hateful to say, both more universal and more persistent in human societies than other bases of discrimination. Slavery was far more destructive of the ability to adapt than European poverty.

Less obviously, there have been major changes in the economy that make it more difficult to break through poverty and its consequences. In earlier periods, the job opportunities for the new immigrants were hard by the old ghettos, in and near the centers of cities. Today, economic activity in metropolitan areas is rapidly decentralizing, and job opportunities are expanding most on the fringes of the urban areas, far removed from the ghettos. Equally important, the character of new job opportunities has been changing. The early waves of immigrants to the cities were able to find unskilled jobs in manufacturing, in construction, and in the transportation industries. Despite poor educational backgrounds, there was a ladder of advancement available; in effect on-the-job training permitted the acquisition of greater skills and better jobs. The ladder was difficult and slippery, but it was there for many.

Today, however, a bigger leap is required. The types of jobs that are most rapidly increasing—in office activities, machine repair and servicing, and other services—tend to have substantial educational requirements. For a variety of reasons, the educational system has been far less successful in equipping the new immigrants than it was in the past. One reason is simply that it is asked to do more—to produce high school, or even college, graduates among the immigrant groups, rather than merely to provide a minimal standard of literacy in the English language. Jobs without substantial educational or skill requirements tend to be in activities and establishments that cannot provide ladders for advancement—the "dead-end" menial jobs paying very low wages.

This can be overstated, for thousands of blacks and Spanish-Americans are in fact continually upgrading their skills and their educational attainments. Perhaps the biggest change lies in the perception of the problems and the opportunities for improvement, both by the minority groups themselves and by the majority of the population. Our society is better able to afford to correct the wretched conditions of life of the new urban immigrants than it was sixty or seventy years ago and is therefore less willing to tolerate them. And most of us are less willing to wait decades for conditions to improve. As the Kerner Commission pointed out:

> . . . nostalgia makes it easy to exaggerate the ease of escape of the white immigrants from the ghettos. . . . [Those] who came to America from rural backgrounds, as Negroes did, are only now, after three generations, in the final stages of escaping from poverty. . . . only the third, and in many cases, only the fourth generation has been able to achieve the kind of middle-class income and status that allows it to send its children to college. . . . Negroes have been concentrated in the city for only two generations, and they have been there under much less favorable conditions.

Housing: Difficulties despite Progress

Housing conditions in urban America have improved tremendously in recent years. In the quarter-century from 1948 through 1972 nearly 40 million new nonfarm houses and apartments were constructed, close to 30 million of these in metropolitan areas. Population has grown rapidly, of course, but the rate of new housing construction has exceeded the rate of population growth.

This has been most striking in the central cities of metropolitan areas, which accounted for only about 8 million of the 60 million increase in the United States population in the twenty-five-year period. The 8 million population increase was matched by an almost equal number of new housing units in the central cities. Because people do not live one person to a housing unit, this permitted great improvements in housing conditions. It has led to the splitting of large households into smaller ones, with much less overcrowding and to demolition of the worst units in the urban housing stock. The new housing has offset destruction by fire and the demolition of urban housing to make room for freeways and other non-residential uses of land.

Even in the largest cities, where population has increased little, if at all, very substantial new housing construction has taken place. As a result, during the 1950s and 1960s, at least 1.5 million "substandard" housing units (units either dilapidated or lacking full plumbing facilities) were eliminated from the housing stock of the dozen largest metropolitan areas, mostly in the central cities. In 1950, roughly 25 percent of the households in all central cities lived in substandard units; by 1968, the figure was cut to only about 4 percent.

Not only has the housing improved, but also huge investments have been made in supporting public and institutional facilities—schools, roads, transit, hospitals, water supply and sewerage, airports, and so on. In the last twenty-five years, over $250 billion has been invested by state and local governments in new public facilities in metropolitan areas, almost as much as the total investment in new housing in these areas during the period. This hardly supports the charge that ours is a society of "public squalor amidst private opulence." Even in the central cities of the North and East, with their slowly growing populations, public outlays for new facilities have been running at the rate of $3 billion annually in recent years, enough to build 50,000 new classrooms each year.

But although we have come a long way since the 1930s

when President Roosevelt could describe one-third of the nation as ill-housed, major housing problems remain, especially for the central-city poor. Although the number of really bad housing units has declined appreciably since then, and 1 million low-rent publicly owned housing units have been built, many blacks and Spanish-speaking Americans are still confined to bad housing. During the 1950s, the number of nonwhites living in substandard housing actually increased. By 1968, nearly 10 percent of all central-city nonwhite households lived in substandard housing, compared to only 3 percent of central-city white households.

In the largest central cities, where the minority populations are concentrated, the situation is even worse, especially if we include "deteriorating" as well as "dilapidated" housing in the slum count. Thus defined, 30 percent or more of the housing occupied by nonwhites in 1960 was slum housing in every American city with a population of over 500,000, except Los Angeles and Washington. In the predominantly black neighborhoods, the situation was even worse. A change in the Census Bureau's system of defining and reporting on housing conditions makes it impossible to update this figure with any precision. But while minority housing conditions in central cities improved substantially during the 1960s, probably reducing the incidence of bad housing among blacks by half or more, there are still a good many black and Hispanic families living in wretched housing in the larger central cities.

The removal of the worst units from the housing stock has sometimes been the result of conscious public policy. However, much of the loss of substandard and even standard housing in the central cities has been the result of a relatively new phenomenon that first became visible in the 1960s,—the large-scale abandonment of rental housing by its owners. An increase in the total supply of housing during the 1950s and

1960s, together with a large-scale decline in central-city populations and, during the late 1960s, in the flow of minority-group immigrants into the cities set the stage for abandonment. In such an environment, owners have found that rents for lower-quality housing located in the most unattractive parts of the ghettos were often insufficient to offset rising taxes, insurance, interest, and maintenance costs. So they cut back on the one cost item they could control, namely, spending for maintenance and repairs. If in addition the neglected housing was in neighborhoods afflicted with exceptionally high crime rates, even low-income tenants would flee the area and the vacant apartments would become prey to vandalism and systematic stripping of plumbing fixtures and other equipment. In this way, large sections, like Woodlawn in Chicago, Brownsville and the South Bronx in New York, and similar neighborhoods in Detroit, Cleveland, Washington, and other cities have in a remarkably brief period become "zones of destruction," abandoned by tenants and landlords alike.[5]

One reason, of course, why rents on low-quality housing cannot be raised readily to meet rising expenses is that the tenants have low incomes and already pay rents that typically are high fractions of their incomes. In most American cities, few white households, except for the elderly and for young single people sharing apartments, spend more than 25 percent of their incomes on housing. But among nonwhite families, rent-income ratios of 35 percent and more are not at all uncommon; in a number of the larger cities, one-third or more of the nonwhite households have such rent-income ratios. Indeed, the need to use so much of a very low income for housing is the principal factor in the cruelly low standard of

5. For a graphic history of the process, see Winston Moore, Charles P. Livermore, and George F. Galland, Jr., "Woodlawn: The Zone of Destruction," *The Public Interest,* no. 30 (Winter 1973).

living of the nonwhite poor in American cities. To a considerable extent, this is why the visible signs of poverty are so much more evident in American than in European cities. The American urban poor have higher incomes than their European counterparts, but must spend far more for housing.

Another visible difference between European cities and the older American cities is found in the deteriorated and decrepit state of so many of the public facilities serving the older parts of the older American cities, despite the high level of expenditure noted previously. As we shall see, the American system of dividing governmental responsibilities places heavy responsibilities on *local* governments, including municipal governments —responsibilities for educating children, alleviating poverty, maintaining law and order, and providing basic community facilities like water supply and sewerage. These responsibilities are only partly matched by money-raising powers. Things are difficult for local governments in general, but in the central cities the difficulties are more severe because the responsibilities of central-city governments are greater than those of other local governments while their ability to tax has diminished over the years. Therefore, it is not surprising that one frequent result is low standards in the maintenance and replacement of public facilities.

There is yet another unpleasant visual aspect of the large, older American cities—their vast neighborhoods of aging, unattractive, and functionally obsolescent housing, neighborhoods that are not slums and are still largely occupied by whites. These neighborhoods have been referred to as "gray areas." They are the neighborhoods that were settled in the first three decades of the twentieth century, with the housing types then popular and suitable—two-family row houses, frame walk-ups, four- or six-story apartment houses, all built with maximum coverage of their sites. These were the neigh-

borhoods opened to settlement by the then-new transit systems (rail and streetcar) and typically occupied then by the
first generation of children of the white immigrants. To them,
it was an escape from the ghettos and a vast improvement in
both their housing and their neighborhood environment.

But such neighborhoods and such housing are no one's first
choice today, and this is true long before any of them become "zones of destruction." In terms of commuting time,
the automobile and the suburban bus and railroad have
brought single-family houses and the openness of the suburbs
almost as close to central-city jobs as the older neighborhoods
are. Increased incomes have permitted subsequent generations
to afford the higher housing and transportation costs of these
more distant but newer residential areas. The old neighborhoods now have only one attraction—lower costs—but this
is not enough in a more affluent age. Thus, the population of
the older neighborhoods ages along with the housing. Because
the housing seems to have little future, except to absorb future
waves of ghetto expansion, owners have little incentive to
maintain their property at high standards. Because the housing was not high quality to begin with (it was designed for a
lower-middle income market), lack of maintenance over long
periods produces real deterioration.

The whole situation is replete with external effects. Everyone might be better off if there were high standards of maintenance and if individual investors replaced the old housing
with new housing. However, the general neighborhood situation is so unattractive that individual property owners feel that
expense for maintenance is too risky and, by withholding
their efforts, contribute to the increasing unattractiveness of
the area. Despite efforts to encourage housing conservation
efforts with the aid of urban renewal funds and by enforcement of housing codes, the "gray areas" remain one of the
unsolved problems of the large older cities.

Expanding ghettos, deteriorating "gray areas," improved transportation to suburban areas, and expanding suburban employment opportunities together have helped the better-off half or two-thirds of the metropolitan population to spread wider and wider. But this spread is not without its costs. The costs include the consumption of large quantities of natural open space in the outer portions of metropolitan areas and the use of an increasing proportion of our national income for urban transportation expenses.

Neither cost would be objectionable, on economic grounds, if the results were the consequences of freely operating individualistic markets, but they are not. In both cases, there are government, as well as individual, decisions; a variety of units and levels of governments are at work; and often the decision makers are not confronted with the costs of their decisions. For example, the costs of suburban highways will be defrayed by statewide and nationwide taxes, not solely from charges paid by suburban highway users. Thus, we cannot be sure that the results are "efficient" in the sense that economists employ that term; the society might be better off with some other combination of resource uses.

Another aspect of urban spread is that it tends to limit the number of "packages" of housing choices. When one buys or rents housing, he chooses a package made up of the housing unit itself, its location relative to his place of work and to other places he wants access to, the characteristics of the neighborhood, and the public services provided in that community. Unless a person is very rich indeed, he must compromise or trade off among price, accessibility, spaciousness, and neighborhood and community characteristics, as we have seen in Chapter 1.

The economic mechanism works best if consumers have a wide array of compromises from which to choose, with relatively small differences among the individual packages; in that way, any individual consumer is likely to be able to come close to his ideal compromise. But the available choices often differ starkly. For example, a moderate-income family may have only three options: (1) a small apartment in a high-density area that is very centrally located; (2) a somewhat larger housing unit in a fairly accessible location, but in an aging neighborhood lacking all sorts of amenities; and (3) a relatively spacious house in a pleasant neighborhood far out on the fringes of the urban area. Typically, such a family chooses the third option, sacrificing a huge amount of accessibility to gain spaciousness and other amenities. The family is unable to gain a small amount of one factor by sacrificing a small amount of another, for no one of the options available permits this kind of compromise.

Of course, the worst limitations on housing choice are those confronted by minority groups suffering from discrimination in housing. If blacks have housing preferences similar to those of whites with the same incomes, particularly in regard to the distances between homes and jobs, many thousands would move outward from the ghettos. An estimate for the mid-1950s suggests that as many as 40,000 black workers in Detroit and 112,000 black workers in Chicago would move out of central ghettos in the absence of racial segregation.[6] The black population of suburban areas did increase in absolute terms during the 1960s, but the racial and economic barriers to suburbanization remain high: only in New York, Los Angeles, and Washington, among the larger metropolitan areas, did the black population of the suburbs increase as a percentage of the total suburban population during the decade.

6. J. R. Meyer, J. F. Kain, and M. Wohl, *The Urban Transportation Problem* (Cambridge, Mass.: Harvard University Press, 1965), Chap. 7.

The Decentralization of Economic Activity

As American cities have increased in size, they have spread outward. The outward spread applies to the location of production, sales, and employment, as well as to the location of housing. There is nothing new about this. It is impossible for all economic activities to be concentrated in the single most centrally located block in a city. From relatively early days in the history of American cities, the rising price of land in the most central locations has tended to sort out economic activities into those that require very central locations and thus can afford to pay the high prices of central land and those whose requirements for centrality are lesser or which need rather large expanses of land. Thus, the farms were forced from Manhattan Island and other central areas; thus, heavy industry covering vast tracts never developed within the old central business districts in the late nineteenth century, but rather outside them.

For years, three interrelated sets of changing circumstances have facilitated the outward movement of economic activity. The first has been improvement in transportation services. In the earliest days, when the forms of land transportation were limited and poor, cities tended to huddle close to waterways, and this was especially true of activities involving a lot of goods handling, notably manufacturing and warehousing. The railroad permitted outward movement of people and economic activity along the rail lines, and the development of urban transit facilities expanded the effective size of central business districts by permitting employers to assemble a labor force at points outside the old centers of activity. The truck, the automobile, and the supporting highway network permitted far more outward movement, not only along the main routes, but in the spaces between them as well.

A second factor in decentralization has been the change in production methods. Again, this was evident even in the early days of urbanization, when steam power freed manufacturing from the waterside locations necessary in the era of water-wheels. It is far more evident now, with the widespread use of production methods requiring spacious single-story plants that cannot be economically developed in built-up central areas but must be located on vacant land at the edges of the de-veloped areas. Changes in communications and data-process-ing technology have also promoted decentralization. Vast numbers of white-collar workers performing repetitive clerical tasks were located in central areas in earlier periods because they could be assembled there most easily and because man-agers and executives could not efficiently utilize the results of their work unless they were all under a single roof. But now this concentration is unnecessary, and the repetitive clerical operations can be located in outlying areas, hooked up to the central offices by computer and other communications systems.

A third factor at work is the change in the nature of "cen-trality" as an urban area grows. This is especially true for the distribution of goods: the old central business district is no longer the most "central" point. It is congested and has little land for expansion of distribution of goods; in addition, the area may be large enough to justify several distribution points, none of them in the very center. The bigger the area and the more dispersed the population, the more likely it is that activi-ties will find the necessary "centrality" outside the central busi-ness district.

Although these forces have been at work for generations, the rate of decentralization has speeded up greatly with the advent of highway transporation and with recent changes in production techniques. In the years since World War II, the rate of decentralization has accelerated to such an extent that it is now a matter of public concern. In part, this is because of the existence of political boundary lines within metropolitan areas. For years, decentralization meant movement from the inner parts of cities to their outer parts, often newly annexed outer parts. More recently the process has been one of movement from central cities to points beyond their boundaries.

Moreover, it is now no longer simply an issue of greater growth in suburbs than in central cities. For many central cities, there have been absolute *declines* in employment in a wide range of activities. For example, between 1958 and 1970, manufacturing employment rose by nearly 3 million in all metropolitan areas. However, in the central cities of the twenty-five largest metropolitan areas, manufacturing employment actually *declined*.

The declines have not been confined to manufacturing. During the past twenty years, central cities in these areas have probably lost a total of 100,000 jobs in wholesale trade, and over 300,000 jobs in retail trade. Both of these movements have been heavily influenced by the spread of the population to the suburbs, as well as by transportation improvements (permitting such developments as the suburban shopping center). Few large central cities, however, have actually experienced declines in total employment. In most cases, the job losses in industry and trade have been offset by job increases in office activities, financial businesses, services, and federal, state, and local government activities. But few large central cities have been able to achieve significant *gains* in total employment.

The decentralization has not been artificial, but has been rather the response of an army of firms to technology and opportunities for low-cost, high-profit production. In this sense, it has been "efficient," but there are serious side effects. Most serious has been the effect, noted earlier, on job opportunities for the poor and untrained, especially members of minority groups. The activities that have been the traditional points of labor-force entry for the urban unskilled—manufacturing, wholesale and retail trade, construction—are precisely those that have been suburbanizing most rapidly, making entry for the central-city poor difficult indeed. The activities expanding in the central cities—office activities, services, government employment—typically have relatively high educational pre-requisites. Not surprisingly, the main beneficiaries of the ex-pansion of such activities have been well-educated whites commuting to the cities from suburban homes.

Another important effect has been on the tax bases of the central cities. Although public services in the cities are increas-ingly supported by federal and state government funds and by local taxes on sales and income, the local property tax remains by far the most important single source of revenue for nearly all cities. Back at the turn of the century, the central cities had virtually a monopoly of the economic activity in their metro-politan areas and thus had available to them a relatively large share of the area's property-tax base. Typically, the central-city property-tax base per capita was a good deal higher than that of suburban areas, until quite recently.

Decentralization has been changing this rapidly. The cities of northern New Jersey (Newark, Jersey City, Paterson, Pas-saic) are typical. By 1955, their tax bases per capita were down to roughly 70 percent of the suburban level; by 1968, the central-city rate had declined to less than 60 percent of the surburban level. During these thirteen years, the tax base increase, in percentage terms, was less than the increase in the prices paid by local governments. This means that the central cities are increasingly *less* able to provide the public services needed by their concentrations of poor blacks and Puerto Ricans.

Although transportation improvements have been a neces-sary condition for the decentralization, the decentralization creates transportation problems. It is far easier to provide adequate transportation service to concentrations of activity, or to activities clustered in the main transportation corridors, than to provide service to a dispersed pattern of locations. For one thing, public transportation can easily link jobs and homes, if one or both ends of the trip are concentrated geographically. With dispersal, public transportation systems have declined in patronage, and increasing reliance must be placed on automobile transportation. The result is very much increased requirements for highways, especially those through built-up suburban areas, where new highway construction means the destruction of high-quality housing. Equally important, the need for auto transportation to work increases the obstacles to job opportunities for the central-city poor, many of whom do not own automobiles.

Quality of the Environment

Social critics frequently assert that a major cost connected with the increasing urban populations is the associated deterioration in the quality of the urban environment, in what we see, hear, drink, and breathe daily. It is not at all clear that American cities are, in an absolute sense, worse off in all these respects than they were say fifty years ago, although they surely are in some respects, such as in regard to the concentrations of air pollutants emitted by motor vehicles and electric power plants. But, in any event, the environment *has* changed, and consciousness of environmental conditions has changed even more.

First, the sheer volume of some pollutants now overwhelms the capacity of the natural environment to assimilate them and render them harmless, probably for the first time in our history.

Second, for some urban residents, particularly among those

who are richer and more articulate, there has been a more
generalized loss, compared to the conditions of life confronting them or their counterparts a generation and more ago.
Third, we are far more aware of how interdependent we are,
of how one group's actions can adversely affect the environment for others, by polluting downstream waters, or increasing
noise levels near airport approaches, or blocking visual access
to waterways. In large part, this is a consequence of urban
growth; an urban society is much more like a self-contained
closed system—a spaceship—than a frontier settlement, where
one can move on to virgin territory when the resources of the
settlement have been exhausted.

Fourth, our aspirations are higher in these regards as in so
many others. Standards of life have risen in most respects. It
is perfectly natural to feel that the noise, dirt, ugliness, and
pollution that were hateful though tolerable years ago are no
longer consistent with our achievements in other areas. And
finally, we know now that our society is rich enough to afford
a better urban environment. In the nineteenth century, we
may not have been able to afford anything better than a narrow interpretation of technological efficiency, so that individual decision makers could and did ignore external effects
on the urban environment. Today we can afford to pay the
higher utility rates resulting from using low-sulfur fuels and
placing utility lines underground or the increased gasoline
taxes required to finance highways located so as to protect
natural open space. In economists' language, the income elasticity of demand for environmental quality appears to be very
high. That is, a poor society is unwilling to surrender much
of its low income for this purpose; but as our incomes rise, we
are willing to devote increasing proportions of income to
measures to improve the environment.

Air and water pollution are good examples of all this. With

a rising urban population and growing economic activity, the sheer volume of pollutants has increased very substantially indeed. Increased numbers and use of motor vehicles have made them the major contributor to the volume of air pollution. But pollution is not new. Prior to the 1950s, all the big northern industrial cities were plagued with the highly visible air pollution caused by the burning of bituminous coal in homes, industry, and steam locomotives; their air was neither healthy nor attractive. Similarly, the rivers and shorefronts near cities, including many smaller ones, have been filthy for decades.

However, a much smaller proportion of the country's population lived in urban areas and therefore only this small group was subjected to the pollution. Moreover, it was more easily avoidable, at least by the richer urban residents, who could live in the pollution-free fringes of cities. Even more important, for the water-pollution problem, communities were less interdependent than they are today. For example, few people may have lived downstream, below the source of pollution. Today, water must be reused much more intensively, for domestic and industrial supply and for recreation, on its way from mountain springs to the sea. Thus, a richer society finds it increasingly appropriate to spend more for pollution control, through taxes to pay for public facilities, through the higher product prices resulting from industrial control efforts, and through other increases in private costs, such as automobile pollution-control devices.

Similar considerations apply to such environmental problems as congestion, noise, dirtiness, and the like. The central parts of American cities were hideously congested years ago, as old photographs show strikingly; the noise and dirt level was by no means low. But a smaller part of the total population was exposed daily to these conditions, and it was easy for the well-off to escape to quiet uncrowded neighborhoods; those who could not escape simply accepted the conditions as unavoidable.

Access to natural open space is another instance in which conditions have changed for some urban residents. For the poor, it was always distant and difficult. For the residents of the outer parts of the cities and of the closest-in suburbs, natural open space was right at hand, often within view. Today, however, the open space within such neighborhoods and immediately beyond them has been filled in by successive waves of suburban development. Natural open space is now distant. It is accessible by improved transportation, but it is not close.

In the case of recreational opportunity, the problem also is, in part, one of distance. The supply of recreational facilities available to urban Americans has been expanding rapidly, and the means of transportation to them have greatly improved. However, the distances one must travel to reach the facilities are increasing, especially if one seeks relatively uncrowded facilities. Shortened workweeks, longer vacations, and high incomes make the demand for recreation a huge one that can be satisfied, at a constant standard of crowding, only by developing new facilities at greater distances. Again here, urban residents used to uncrowded facilities close at hand have experienced a deterioration in environmental quality. A further complication is the intense demand for sites for nonrecreational uses in close-in areas; recreational land is frequently sought for such purposes.

Beauty in land and buildings has always been highly prized by the richest of city-dwellers throughout the world. But a good deal of surrounding ugliness for the poor was usually accepted as inevitable. This was especially true of the cities that grew rapidly during the great industrial age in the nineteenth century in Europe and in America. In this country, some

of the ugliest residential building types known to man dominated the period of rapid city building between 1870 and
1930—the "Old Law tenements" in New York and their
counterparts in other northeastern cities; the miles of closely
spaced frame houses in midwestern cities; the row houses and
shoulder-to-shoulder apartment buildings of the 1920s. Urban
ugliness seems a more serious problem now because of the
mass and density of city building and the disappearance of
open space. Big, ugly buildings are worse than small ones, and
unrelieved masses much worse than concentrations broken by
open space and by intervening stretches of small attractive
structures. Most important of all, here too we can afford to
do much better. We are, after all, much richer than the Flor-
ence of the Medicis, the London of the eighteenth-century
ducal developers, and the Paris of Napoleon III.

So, it is really not important to determine how fast the
urban environment is, in fact, deteriorating in an absolute
sense. There is increasing dissatisfaction with environmental
quality, increasing realization that it is more difficult than ever
for individuals to escape the noxious aspects of the urban
environment, and increasing conviction that it is within the
economic power of our society to do something about the
problems.

Getting around in Cities

During the 1960s, government spent over $3 billion a year
for new urban highways and over $200 million a year for
improvements in transit facilities and equipment, not to men-
tion hundreds of millions more for operating and maintaining
urban transportation facilities and services. The investment in
urban highways has produced hundreds of miles of high-
capacity expressways in urban areas, roads carrying as many

as 100,000 vehicles a day, opening new areas to development for housing, and permitting, for the first time in their histories, swift movement within the built-up portions of many large cities. At the same time, publicly and privately owned transit systems have been purchasing thousands of new buses and hundreds of new subway and suburban rail cars.

Despite all this, there seems to be a widespread impression that difficulties in getting around in cities worsen continually in the large metropolitan areas. Among the complaints frequently read or heard are these:

- Despite all the road building, journeys to work take as long or longer than ever and, in many cases, increased travel time has offset shortened working hours over the last generation.
- The vastly expensive urban expressways are really quite useless, because they are crowded beyond their capacities at rush hours as soon as they are opened; the New York area's Long Island Expressway has been called "the world's longest parking lot."
- Weekend and holiday traffic jams are even worse than those of weekday rush hours, making the new roads and bridges "useless" for recreation travel as well.
- Public transportation equipment and service is deteriorating, yet rush-hour buses and trains are more crowded than ever before.

To a considerable extent, the complaints are founded on a lagging perception of the changes that have actually been occurring. The worst traffic jams are those that occur during major construction jobs; and actual completion of urban expressway *systems,* rather than segments, is only now being achieved, fifteen years after the rate of construction activity was massively stimulated by initiation of the federal interstate highway program. The acceleration in the rate of transit improvements is even newer, after twenty years or more in which little net investment took place in most large cities. Often, the critics have not caught up with the fact that transit systems have completely replaced their vehicles and rolling stock.

Then, too, some of the criticisms are erroneous in a quantitative sense. Journeys to work take a long time in large part because people travel much longer distances from home to job. The new expressways may be jammed at peak travel hours, but often on the parallel streets and roads that previously were snarled traffic now flows freely. Moreover, the investment in new roads is surely not worthless if the new facilities carry many more people longer distances, even if not very rapidly at the peak hours. A system that accommodates a million daily trips averaging eight miles in length has a very substantially higher output than one that handles 800,000 trips averaging six miles. Similarly, the weekend traffic volumes are enormously larger. It is not a failure of the urban transportation system that accounts for the crowding of previously uncrowded highways on winter Sunday evenings in the Northeast, but rather the greatly increased popularity of skiing.

However, the dissatisfaction is not all imaginary. There is room for doubt as to whether the vast investment in new facilities has been optimal—whether the allocation of effort among the modes of transportation has been right, whether the right projects have been selected, whether the projects have been properly executed, and whether there are not alternative ways of dealing with the problems. For example, the urban expressway program in a number of cities has been slowed or stopped dead by increased opposition to highways that slash through built-up areas destroying neighborhoods or violate natural open space areas.

The major issue in recent years is whether too much emphasis has been placed on facilitating automobile transportation in urban areas, relative to improvements in public transportation modes—bus, subway, suburban railroad. Despite the huge increase in the American urban population, patronage of public transportation has declined tremendously in the past generation. The number of fare-paying passengers is now only 40 percent of the 1950 level; it is little more than 50 percent of the 1940 level. Most of the decline occurred in the first fifteen years following World War II; since 1960, patronage of subway and suburban rail systems has been fairly stable, but city bus patronage continues to drop.

This has been mainly the result of the underlying changes in the distribution of population and jobs, combined with the rise in incomes that permits people to afford the higher cost, but greater flexibility and comfort, of automobile transportation. The dispersal of the population to new suburban areas not well served by public transportation lines clearly goes hand in glove with greater auto ownership and use. The decentralization of economic activity is similar; dispersed suburban job locations simply cannot be readily served by public transportation, which requires concentrations of passenger traffic along a relatively few routes if it is to succeed economically.

But in addition there has been some element of what economists call "market failure." Changing transportation patronage is partly the result of the failure of the mechanisms through which consumer choice is exercised to reflect properly the costs and other conditions that should govern consumer choice. This is to be expected where there is so much governmental participation, as there is in transportation, and indeed governmental participation is often designed to change the factors to which consumers respond. However, at least some of the market failure appears to be accidental, rather than intentional.

No urban transportation services are offered to users free of charges. There are transit fares and charges on motorists arising from highway use, mainly tolls and gasoline taxes. In neither case does the structure of charges present the proper signals to individual consumers who must decide how they are to travel. The proper signals, from an economic standpoint, would tell each user how much each use of the service is costing society, that is, what the opportunity costs of the consumer's decision will be. On balance, this element of market failure has unduly encouraged consumers to use their automobiles for peak-hour trips to and from the central sections of larger cities.

Also, the complicated patterns of financing transportation (different levels of government and public-private mixes) have produced differential access to funds for expanding, improving, and modernizing transportation services and facilities. These "imperfections in the capital markets," as economists style them, have very much favored highways as against transit. Large sums of federal and state government money have been available for the former. The latter have had to reply on hard-pressed municipal governments and near-bankrupt private transit companies and suburban railroads. The lack of capital and the declines in patronage have contributed to the technological backwardness of public transportation—offering speeds and standards of comfort and efficiency that have changed little in fifty years to compete with new automobiles and expressways. This, of course, has speeded the competitive decline of public transportation.

The resulting imbalance in urban transportation modes presents two major problems, both of which are of special importance for the larger central cities. One is the extreme costliness and political and social difficulty (which are other kinds of costs) of trying to provide adequate highway capacity in and near the central business districts and through the older, close-in suburbs to handle the rush-hour traffic flows. Recognition of this factor, more than any other, is responsible for the revival of public concern with transit and for governmental efforts to redress the imbalance—federal aid for mass transit, large-scale state government efforts in the northeastern states, and large local government tax support for public transportation in San Francisco Bay area, among other places.

The second problem is the impact of the decline in public transportation service on those groups among whom auto ownership is uncommon. In the United States, 80 percent of the households own automobiles; in practice, automobile ownership is nearly universal except among the very poor and the elderly. In 1972, 42 percent of households whose head was sixty-five years old or older and about 40 percent of younger households with incomes below $5,000 did not own automobiles; the percentages are apparently substantially higher within central cities. Among black households 45 percent did not own cars. The patronage of only these groups in the urban population is unlikely to be sufficient to financially support robust public transportation service. But inadequate service leaves these groups stranded, without access to better jobs or to community facilities and services on which the poor, elderly, and disadvantaged must rely heavily. In a narrow sense, it is inefficient to plan, build, and operate urban transportation systems for such groups, but in a broader sense, reflecting the common responsibility for the less fortunate, it is not at all certain where efficiency lies.

The Urban Fiscal Problem

Most of the country's state, county, municipal, and school district governments serving urban areas have been making enormous efforts to mobilize public funds to cope with urban problems. During the past twenty-five years, state and local government has been the most rapidly growing sector of the national economy. The country's total output of goods and services—the gross national product—is now more than three times as great as it was twenty years ago, but state-local government expenditure (nearly two-thirds of which occurs in metropolitan areas) is more than six times as great as it was then. Public outlays have been increased by a rising price level and by the need to provide for a larger population, but that is not the whole explanation, for local government expenditure has been climbing rapidly even in central cities with declining populations. What has been happening is that the scope and quality of state-local government services have been greatly enhanced.

When one sector of the economy expands more rapidly than the economy as a whole, the rapidly expanding sector is in the process withdrawing resources from the other sectors. Governments manage this resource transfer primarily through taxation—compulsory payments by consumers and businesses to government that increase the purchasing power of the latter and reduce the purchasing power of the former. State and local governments have been increasing their taxes and adopting new ones at a high rate during the past twenty years.

The most important state government tax is the sales tax. By 1972, forty-five states had sales taxes that averaged about 4 percent; this form of taxation is also used by more than 4,000 local governments in twenty-six states. But back in 1945, only twenty-four states imposed sales taxes, usually at a 2 percent rate, and New York and New Orleans were the only cities in the country to use this tax. The individual income tax is used by forty state governments and by local governments in nine states; in 1945, thirty-two states used the tax, at lower rates, and Philadelphia was the only city with an income tax. During the past twenty years, there has been an enormous increase in the market value of taxable property in American urban areas, but property-tax collections have increased half again as much, substantially increasing the burden of the tax, especially in central cities.

Because tax increases reduce the purchasing power of individuals and businesses, they have been hotly fought, despite the wide attraction of the additional public services the tax increases finance. There is simultaneously increased voter resistance to tax rises and an increased appreciation that the unmet needs, which governments can try to satisfy, are so great.

The dilemma is sharpest in the large central cities. Governments serving the central cities have great responsibilities for coping with the problems of race and poverty. They must spend huge sums for public assistance, health services to the poor, and a variety of similar although less costly services merely to alleviate the visible symptoms. If they are to contribute to the eradication of poverty, they must do still more, especially to raise educational attainment and to eliminate substandard housing conditions. Although more money pure and simple is not the sole answer, it is reasonable to suppose that governments serving the large, old central cities could usefully spend much more than they are now spending to provide public services needed because there are large concentrations of the poor in the cities.

At the same time, central-city governmental units have been making great efforts to improve the livability of the cities, for poor and middle-class people alike—by improving transportation services, by expanding recreational opportunity, by reducing air and water pollution, and by replacing deteriorated public facilities of all sorts. In combination, the pressure for increased expenditure is severe.

This might not be so severe a problem if we lived with quite different governmental arrangements. In the United States, we have traditionally expected the local governments to be the main providers of urban public services, with a lesser (although still important role) for state governments. The relative importance of local governments as a provider of public services is greater in the United States than in any other major country, except Canada. In most other countries, the national government has a much greater role in the provision of health and welfare services, in transportation, in higher education, and in other fields. The difficulty with the American system is that the higher levels of government are inherently much better tax collectors than are the lower levels, for the high levels can tax a broad segment of income and wealth rather than only the small pieces within local boundaries, and they can effect economies of scale in tax collection—more equipment, more technical personnel, and so forth.

We adapt to this imbalance between service responsibilities and revenue-raising capabilities by providing grants from the higher to the lower levels. However, the grants have not resolved the imbalance. As a result, central-city governments must rely heavily on their own tax-raising capacities. But the decentralization of economic activity in urban areas has tended to undermine central-city tax bases, as noted earlier. The central cities have a smaller piece of the metropolitan economic pie than in earlier years. The inevitable response—to increase tax rates on a slowly growing tax base—can make things worse. Typically, central-city tax instruments bear harshly on the central-city poor (especially the property tax on housing). Equally important, they can speed the departure to the suburbs of central-city business activity and of the higher-income people still living in the central cities.

The suburbs, too, are experiencing great fiscal stress. In part, these are growing pains. The rapid transformation of rural areas with low public service requirements into built-up suburbs typically inhabited by families with children of school age enormously increases public expenditure and local tax levels and does so almost overnight. The increased tax level is especially hard on the earliest residents, who settled in the community with expectations of a semirural, low-tax environment.

In addition, there is a serious problem arising from the heterogeneity of suburban fiscal resources. Not surprisingly, new suburbanites attracted by the good schools and community amenities that characterize the rich suburbs developed a generation or more ago—the Scarsdales, Highland Parks, Newtons —aspire to similar public services. However, not all the new suburbs are enclaves of the very rich. Most are middle-income communities, and some are on the low side of that middle range. Moreover, some have large amounts of business property to tax—industrial plants, shopping centers, and the like —and some are virtually entirely residential.

As a result, the better-off places are able to provide superior services at lower tax rates. And there is a powerful incentive to try to preserve the favored position, or to move toward it, by controlling the pattern of development—by zoning out moderate-income families with their hordes of school children and zoning in business property, which pays taxes, but has no school children. The resulting land-use pattern of the metropolitan area is neither efficient nor equitable, because neither efficiency nor equity are criteria used in the planning decisions of thousands of individual suburban governments.

Conclusion

As varied and severe as the problems of American urban areas are, it can be argued that most of the problems with an economic dimension are actually becoming less serious in a measurable, quantitative sense. The incidence of urban poverty *is* declining, and the economic status of urban minorities is improving; the quality and quantity of the housing stock is getting better, not worse; there is far more concern for, and action to improve, environmental quality than ever before; immense improvements in urban transportation facilities are in the works; and governments are raising and spending vastly greater amounts to solve urban problems.

Some critics have observed the improvements and commented that the reformers and dissenters are out of touch with the economic realities, that the complaints really refer to conditions of a decade and more ago, and that the majority of urban Americans are really quite satisfied with urban America. All this may be true. But those who really do suffer, the central-city poor in their racial ghettos, know as well as the reformers that we have the economic capacity to do much more. The remainder of this book is devoted to an economic examination of the policies designed to do more.

PART II

POLICY OPTIONS

3

Dealing with Urban Poverty

As the discussion in Chapter 2 has suggested, there are several distinguishable (although interrelated) causes for the existence of large concentrations of low-income people in the central parts of large urban areas—which is defined here as *the* urban poverty problem. Each of these causes calls for a somewhat different combination of policy solutions, and so the overall policy package that one advocates will depend upon one's assessment of the relative importance of the various causes of the problem. It will also depend upon one's time horizons, that is, how badly we desire immediate rather than long-run solutions. Some antipoverty policies will begin to work as soon as they are adopted, whereas others can have effects only over fairly lengthy periods—some as long as ten to fifteen years.

A central concern of urban economists is, or should be, the extent to which the characteristic spatial distribution of economic activities in large urban areas creates shortages of employment opportunities for many city residents. The increasing suburbanization of economic activities, for example, limits job opportunities for the poor, particularly the minority-group

71

poor, who for the most part continue to live in the central cities. Moreover, the job opportunities that remain in central locations tend to be either high-skilled ones, for which many central area residents are ill-equipped, or very low paying ones that do not provide enough money to meet the high costs of central-area housing and to maintain the large families that are so frequently characteristic of low-income households. To the extent that the spatial distribution of activities is the cause of the urban poverty problem, the policies called for involve changing the location of jobs and/or people and improving the skills of low-income people who remain in central areas.

Reducing poverty by policies that improve the access of the poor to more and better-paid jobs is of course in accord with the traditional American preference for linking the receipt of income to contributions to the nation's output. Another type of antipoverty policy also has a long tradition behind it, but it is the Western world's tradition of charity, not work: alleviate or eliminate poverty by providing direct income-maintenance payments to those poor who cannot benefit from employment programs for one reason or another. Obviously, more weight should be placed upon income-maintenance policies in those cases where the poverty problem does not arise from the spatial maldistribution of jobs, housing, and skill endowments, but rather from other causes. A major such cause is the increase in households headed by females in large cities, particularly households with numerous young children. Another is the stranding of low-income elderly people, too poor to migrate, in the central parts of large cities that in many ways are peculiarly unsuitable locations for older people: for example, rents are high, their exposure to crime and violence is considerable, and they must depend on public transportation systems designed for the young and agile.

Employment, housing, and training policies can have only a limited role in dealing with urban poverty that is related to family structure and family life-cycles. Here the problem is to devise suitable income transfer policies and at the same time minimize the creation of family units that are not economically viable. As we shall see, the problem is an exceptionally difficult one that has not yet been solved.

Before we examine these policy alternatives at greater length, it is important to note a rather fundamental disagreement among urban economists regarding the overall direction of national policies concerned with urban poverty. Some have argued that *any* set of policies designed to improve the economic circumstances of the poor within the large central cities is likely to be self-defeating. Despite the heavy migration of blacks, Chicanos, and Puerto Ricans from rural areas to the large cities, there still are large numbers of potential migrants to the cities among the rural poor, both in the mainland United States, and Puerto Rico and Latin America. Thus, any substantial *differential* improvements within the large cities— more jobs, better housing opportunities, improvement in the public-assistance payments available only in the urbanized northern and western states—are likely to attract so many more poor people that conditions in the cities will improve only marginally. According to these economists, the appropriate way to deal with urban poverty is to accelerate economic development in the poorer regions (particularly in the smaller cities in those regions) and to increase income-maintenance payments in those areas relative to the public assistance available in northern and western cities. This will retain population in the poorer regions and truly improve their lot, while permitting longer-term natural economic growth and suburbanization to improve the lot of the poor now in the large cities.[1]

---

1. See John F. Kain and Joseph J. Persky, "Alternatives to the Gilded Ghetto," *The Public Interest,* no. 14 (Winter 1969).

However, the statistical evidence indicates clearly that those who migrate from rural to urban areas do improve their economic circumstances, and markedly so. In 1971, there were 400,000 fewer poor black families in the United States than in 1959, although the total number of black families had increased by 1.3 million. The entire increase in the number of black families occurred in metropolitan areas, but there was no increase in the number of poor black families in metropolitan areas. In effect, therefore, the migration to metropolitan areas removed 400,000 black families from poverty. Migration appears to improve the housing conditions of low-income households to an even greater extent, moreover.

It is true that the migration of the poor to the cities tends to preclude any large reduction in the number of poor families within the cities, but it is impossible to ignore the benefits to those who migrate. Thus, most urban economists continue to support "ghetto-gilding" policies, on the grounds that, in the aggregate, increasing urbanization makes things better, not worse, for large numbers of people.

Employment Policies

The basic argument for employment policies rests on the observation that even when the economy as a whole is booming, unemployment rates among urban Negroes (and among the urban Hispanic minorities) are high—at least twice as high as among similar age groups of whites. A booming economy, in other words, does not automatically eliminate unemployment among the minority groups that comprise so large a share of the urban poor, and particularly among younger males in the minority groups. This is one form of what economists call "structural unemployment." Overall, the demand for labor may be high in boom periods, but the supply of minority-group labor is not well matched to the available jobs. As suggested earlier, this mismatch has a number of facets. One is geography. The most rapid increase in jobs for people who have modest skills occurs in the suburbs, whereas the minority-group poor live in the central cities, far from the expanding job opportunities.

A second, and perhaps even more important, aspect is the mismatch of skills. In a boom period, the modern economy has a great demand for all sorts of highly skilled persons and for people with educational backgrounds that enable them to learn new skills easily. The minority-group poor do not possess these skills; they are in the market for the relatively unskilled jobs that the economy does not supply in abundance. To bridge these gaps, two sets of policies have been advanced and are being pursued. These two sets of policies are, in concept, contradictory. In practice they are not mutually exclusive. One set of policies seeks to bring the job to the ghettos; the other seeks to bring the ghetto residents to jobs, both geographically and by changing the skill and educational endowments of ghetto residents.

A large variety of plans for expanding employment opportunities within, or on the fringes of, the ghettos of large cities (especially those in the Northeast) have been advanced. Some of the plans are not at all revolutionary, but simply attempt to reproduce, in today's ghettos, forms of economic development that have worked well in the American economy in the past.

One such approach is to foster the development of small businesses owned and operated by Negroes and other minority-group people within the ghettos. Usually, these are retail and consumer-service businesses. The assumption is that, despite the low income levels in the ghettos, consumer demand is adequate to support better consumer-oriented services than are now provided. Thus, programs have been developed to provide easier credit and management training to minority-group small businessmen, to enable them to take over existing small businesses, expand existing establishments, and start entirely new businesses.

A highly imaginative proposal for black small-business ownership, not confined to ghetto locations, has been advanced by Anthony Pascal. He suggests that blacks need an economic "turf" of their own, as a platform for economic advancement, much in the way that successful ethnic minority groups in the past achieved dominance in an industry or economic specialty—the Italians in construction, the Irish in urban local government, the Jews in communications and the garment trade, to cite the most obvious examples. His candidate as the appropriate economic turf for blacks is the gasoline service station business, and he proposes a program to transfer ownership of large numbers of the 220,000 gas stations in the United States to black proprietors over time.[2]

But, however worthy, small businesses cannot provide the million or so new jobs needed to eliminate unemployment and underemployment in the ghettos. Today, most large central cities actively encourage sizeable industrial enterprises to locate in or near the ghettos—through industrial promotion programs that provide assistance in getting credit, locating industrial sites, and avoiding city government red tape—in an attempt to expand the supply of jobs available to ghetto residents.

Much more ambitious and expensive schemes have been proposed for adoption by the federal government. One such scheme would involve the use of federal tax credits to encourage major national corporations to build plants and

---

2. Anthony H. Pascal, "Black Gold and Black Capitalism," *The Public Interest*, no. 19 (Spring 1970).

employ people within the ghettos. The idea is that these corporations pay large amounts of federal taxes on their other activities, and if there were big tax savings to be derived from investing in the ghettos they would be unable to pass up these opportunities.

Similarly, there are proposals for, and experiments with, the direct payment of federal wage subsidies to firms that locate their plants within the ghettos and hire a minimum number of minority-group people. Another type of job-creation scheme calls for a vast expansion of ghetto housing construction using manpower recruited from the ghettos. And recent federal housing legislation does encourage the use of local labor. The idea here is that the housing and rehabilitation is worthwhile in its own right and that a very large expansion of housing construction activity will lower the traditional union barriers to minority-group entrants into the building trades and thus provide a natural ladder of advancement to high-paid jobs through on-the-job training.

The whole concept of bringing jobs to the ghettos has been severely criticized. Such policies are said to run counter to the powerful decentralizing trend in American metropolitan areas. It is much harder to buck a strong economic trend than to figure out some way to ride with it. In many of the ghettos, moreover, population density is high, and there is little vacant land. Construction of factories or other enterprises that require a lot of land would aggravate existing housing problems in some areas and would be resented by ghetto residents. Finally, in the light of all these obstacles and the "unnatural" character of such efforts, the kinds of industries most likely to be recruited for a ghetto economic development program would tend to be industries paying relatively low wages and offering limited chances for advancement, and the firms themselves might very well be highly unstable. This criticism suggests that ghetto economic development is at best a temporary kind of device because it seems unlikely to help resolve the very large and long-term problem of low-wage employment.

At this point it is important to keep in mind that a very significant part of poverty in American cities relates not to unemployment but to the low wages earned by adult male heads of households. In a recent study, it was found that of all the people living in poverty (as officially defined) in American metropolitan areas in 1968 about 25 percent belonged to households headed by adult males below the age of sixty-five who actually had jobs.[3] They *were* employed, although in many cases sporadically, during the course of the year, but almost without exception at very low wages. Another 13 percent of all persons living in poverty were in households in which there was an adult male head under the age of sixty-five, but without a job at all. Bringing jobs to the ghetto would tend to reduce the second class of problems, unemployment for the adult male, but might not do much for the males employed at low wages. (The massive housing-construction proposal is an exception to this observation because, apart from providing housing, it could also provide greater access to better-paying jobs.)

THE GEOGRAPHIC GAP

One way in which the geographic gap between ghetto residents and jobs in the economically expanding outer parts of the metropolitan area can be bridged is to provide better transportation. For the very poor who cannot afford automobiles, this means expanding or improving public transpor-

---

3. Anthony Downs, *Who Are the Urban Poor?* Committee for Economic Development, Supplementary Paper 26, rev. ed., September 1970.

tation services. Unfortunately, this is very difficult, because suburban job locations are frequently dispersed over a wide area and not concentrated as they are in central cities. Buses and trains cannot provide access to plants scattered over the suburban landscape, except at high fares and with slow service.

But there are some cases in which suburban job opportunities are concentrated, and in these cases improved public transportation service can help to make them accessible to ghetto residents. In the few large metropolitan areas with suburban rail systems (New York, Chicago, Philadelphia, Boston, and San Francisco are the main ones), ghetto residents might use these systems in larger numbers if only the fares were lower. Economics suggests moreover that the fares should be low, because the ghetto residents would be commuting on largely empty trains, traveling *away from* the central cities in the mornings and *toward* the central cities in the evenings, in the opposite directions that the thousands of suburban commuters travel. If a train is largely empty, the opportunity cost—the cost in real resources—of carrying extra passengers is very close to zero. This is a case in which large social benefits might be realized if ways were found to deal with the money, not the real, costs of railroad operations.

Even now, in some metropolitan areas, there is a considerable volume of "reverse commuting" from the central-city minority-group areas to outlying plants, often on the basis of car pooling. For example, the Ford plant in suburban Mahwah, New Jersey, employs large numbers of central-city Negroes. During rush hours, traffic flow on the George Washington Bridge connecting New York City and suburban New Jersey is nearly equal in both directions. Many of the reverse commuters live in central-city ghettos and work in suburban plants.

The transportation solution to ghetto employment problems

has been severely criticized. For one thing, distances in the larger metropolitan areas are very great, and, even with good transportation, it means asking ghetto residents to spend a large amount of time—*and* money—on travel. In American metropolitan areas there are many people who travel great distances, spending a lot of time and money to get between their jobs and homes, but this is closely related to the level of wages and salaries—the higher the earnings level, the more likely people are to travel long distances at high costs. But, the ghetto residents for whom these policies are designed would presumably be earning fairly modest amounts of money.

Moreover, better transportation does not solve one major disadvantage resulting from the separation of ghettos from suburban jobs: knowledge of job openings. In our society this is to a considerable extent a word-of-mouth, casual kind of thing. Logically, the next step in bringing ghetto residents to the job is not by improving transportation but by providing them with housing in the suburban areas where job opportunities are expanding rapidly. Indeed, official policy outlawing discrimination in housing is aimed in that direction. But, however desirable, there are many obstacles to this kind of policy, from the high price of much suburban housing to discrimination per se.

THE SKILL GAP

Another way to bring ghetto residents to the jobs is to upgrade their skills and to match them better for the jobs that are in fact available. Many of these job openings are in central business districts of the large cities, not only in the suburbs. Large firms are increasingly providing specialized training programs for ghetto residents, and in fact there exist a wide range of training programs in operation right now along with very substantial federal government expenditure for man-power training and development. Such federal programs enrolled roughly a million persons a year in the late 1960s and early 1970s. Public and private job training is not new, of course. On-the-job training, apprenticeship arrangements, and vocational schools are all well-established institutions. What is new is the recognition of the difficulty and cost of successfully training and advancing people who have not succeeded in formal schooling, have little work experience (and thus no work habits), and have had little hope of getting and keeping well-paid jobs with opportunities for betterment.

This has led to the "street academies" for high-school dropouts, a variety of programs attached to the ghetto schools, and entirely new kinds of on-the-job training schemes. One of the most extensive and expensive of these involves federal grants of up to $4,000 per employee to private firms training and guaranteeing jobs to the "hard core" of unemployed ghetto residents; the training program includes prejob remedial work, plus on-the-job training. Because a failure rate of 50 percent or more is not unusual, the costs per successful worker are very high. But the benefits can be very large indeed—the training program may increase the lifetime earnings prospects of a twenty-year-old youth by $200,000 or more.[4]

Another component of a policy designed to bridge the skill gap is to reexamine the requirements for particular jobs. Are

---

4. A twenty-year-old ghetto resident may very well look forward to a lifetime of intermittent, low-wage employment with earnings averaging $3,000 a year. The training program might equip him for a lifetime of steady employment at annual earnings averaging $8,000 or more. The $5,000 average difference works out to $225,000 over the forty-five years from age twenty to age sixty-five. Discounted at an interest rate of 7 percent, the present value of the incremental income stream is roughly $68,000, several times the cost of the training program (even if there is a very high failure rate and, thus, high costs per successful completion).

they really essential or do they merely serve to bar ghetto residents from the jobs? For example, many male adolescents in the ghettos accumulate police records for minor infractions that may render them unemployable. Some firms are experimenting with new employment arrangements that overlook these minor infractions. Other firms are asking whether a high-school diploma is in fact necessary for some of their entering jobs.

Still another approach to the skills gap is to see whether some of the jobs that are now available could not be broken down into less skilled components. In the health field, for example, jobs that have been traditionally reserved for highly trained professionals are being increasingly filled by less trained people.[5] Yet another way to bring ghetto residents to the jobs that exist is to improve the efficiency of the employment agencies, public and private, so that ghetto residents have better information about the jobs that are in fact available.

A wholly different type of employment solution to the urban poverty problem is to have the government set itself up as the employer of last resort for all those persons willing and able to work but unable to find jobs in the private sector. The justification for this approach is that many services that only government can provide need improvement very badly—health services, maintenance and repair of public structures of all kinds, and so on. To permit these services to go unprovided while there are unemployed persons capable of doing the job,

---

5. In a study in New York City, it was estimated that as many as 25,000 new career positions in city government services (particularly health services) could be created by job redesign, to employ the poor and fill existing professional and technical job vacancies. Mark A. Haskell, "The Public Sector and Employment of the Poor," New York University, Graduate School of Business Administration, (New York, June 1968).

so runs the argument, is to be completely bemused by a money illusion. That is, while governments may say they cannot afford the *money* costs of such services, the *resource* costs to society as a whole are very small or even nil. What would have been done with the unemployed labor resources had government not stepped in as employer of last resort? The answer is, of course, that the resources—unemployed people—would have been unused, and therefore the opportunity cost is zero, or very close to it.

There are, however, difficulties with this idea. Any expansion of government programs, even when costless in resource terms, is likely to involve the levying of additional taxes, which are never painless. A more important objection is that the types of jobs that would be made available would be mainly jobs that will always be low-skilled, relatively low-paid jobs.

Moreover, in order to meet their commitments as employer of last resort, governments would be encouraged to be labor-intensive, to refrain from automating and to use labor instead of machinery. That would be highly inefficient. The ultimate scarce resource everywhere is the number of hours that people can devote to productive jobs over their working lives. To put people to work in a way that maximizes low-productivity uses of their time and to refrain from innovating and mechanizing wherever possible, is a very backward step indeed. In other parts of the world, typically in poorer countries, we do have examples of permanent overstaffing of government so as to maximize employment opportunities. The result is not satisfactory incomes for government employees, a high rate of economic growth for the society, or adequate levels of government service.

These are arguments against an *open-ended* commitment for government to act as employer of last resort, creating jobs whether or not there is work to be done. A more limited commitment, to avoid a money illusion and put unemployed people to work providing public services where this can be usefully done, has much to say for it. And there are federal programs encouraging this. Under legislation adopted in the late 1960s and implemented vigorously during the 1970–1971 recession, the federal government will pay up to 90 percent of the salaries of previously unemployed people put to work in new state and local government jobs that have opportunities for advancement.

Yet another employment policy strategy concerns the level of the minimum wage. As was noted earlier, over one-fourth of the poverty problem in American cities is related to low-wage employment. If the minimum wage is $2 an hour, a person who works forty hours per week and fifty weeks per year has an annual income of $4,000. This was just about the poverty income threshold for a four-person household in 1970. Workers who receive the minimum wage and have families with more than four members will be, according to the official definition, in poverty; a very substantial number of the households that are in poverty in American cities are large households. Therefore, some people argue that we should raise the minimum wage to a level that will permit a fully employed adult male to earn enough so that he and his family will not be below the very low, official poverty line.

This argument runs up against the classic case against minimum wages in general. There are both people whose productivity is very low and jobs that are barely worthwhile, from the firm's standpoint. Raise the minimum wage and the jobs simply will not be filled or the persons simply will not be employed. Without a doubt, increases in the minimum wage do increase unemployment. For example, extension of minimum-wage provisions to agricultural laborers in recent years has thrown a good many farm workers in the Deep South out of jobs.

One way around this problem is to retain minimum-wage laws, but provide for wage subsidies to employers of low-skilled people. As a matter of fact, we do operate our social security and unemployment insurance systems today on the basis of taxes on payrolls, and these are in effect negative subsidies. It is easy to conceive of a wage subsidy scheme that works in the opposite direction and makes higher minimum wages feasible, without increasing unemployment. One specific argument for such an arrangement is that many of the low-wage, dead-end jobs in an urban economy are in combination essential to its functioning, although the contribution of each such job to total output is small, and so its wage is low. If such jobs are truly essential, people must be provided with adequate monetary incentives to do them. If the income-maintenance system is made more adequate, the required incentives for unattractive jobs will be higher.

Income–Maintenance Policies

Nearly one-fourth of all the urban poor are either elderly or members of households headed by a disabled adult male. Close to one-third are in households headed by a female under the age of sixty-five with children. Together these figures suggest that close to half of all the urban poor are people who cannot be directly helped by employment policies. These are people who are very unlikely to be members of the labor force. The only way that they can be helped here and now is to provide them with more income through direct payments from the government, payments not connected with jobs. Moreover, even for some of those who can some day become successful self-sustaining members of the labor force, income-maintenance programs make sense, because their successful participation in the labor force may be some time off, after the completion of lengthy training programs.

In the United States, governments have operated income-maintenance programs from the earliest days. However, until the onset of the depression in the 1930s, income maintenance consisted largely of local relief activities for the aged and other indigent groups; often these activities consisted of little more than supporting the indigent in old peoples' homes and poor farms. Mass destitution in the 1930s led to passage of the Social Security Act in 1935, establishing the social security system and providing federal grants for state government unemployment insurance and public assistance programs. In 1971, about $75 billion was spent for income-maintenance payments: public-assistance (welfare) payments; social security benefits to retired persons, surviving dependents of deceased workers, and the disabled; unemployment insurance benefits; disability compensation and pensions to veterans; and workman's compensation payments for work-connected injuries and diseases.

As Table 3-1 shows, in 1970 about 25 million persons benefited from programs aimed at the retired and the elderly; 5 million people received payments under programs connected with disability; and more than 15 million people, many of them children, received payments because families had been broken by death or desertion or because of the unemployment of the family's wage earner.[6]

The problem with the existing programs is that they simply do not do an adequate job; moreover, in some cases they have objectionable side effects. Despite the more than $75 billion spent, they leave many Americans in poverty. In 1966, 20

---

6. The total number of beneficiaries from the programs was significantly less than 45 million, because some people receive payments from more than one program.

percent of our population—almost 39 million people—were in families whose private incomes were below the poverty level. Even after receiving the various available government income-maintenance payments, there were still 28.5 million people in families with incomes below the poverty level. Thus,

TABLE 3-1 *Beneficiaries of Major Income-Maintenance Programs, 1970*

	Millions of Beneficiaries
1. Payments to households headed by older and retired people:	
Social Security and Railroad Retirement	21
Public Assistance	2
Veterans Programs	3
2. Payments to younger households connected with disability:	
Social Security and Railroad Retirement	2
Public Assistance	1
Veterans Programs	2
3. Payments to younger households connected with death, absence, or unemployment of head of household:	
Social Security and Railroad Retirement	5
Public Assistance	10
Veterans Programs	1
Unemployment Insurance Programs	2

Source: Adapted from *Statistical Abstract of the United States*, 1972.

the income-maintenance programs reduced the numbers of poor people by less than 30 percent. The programs did not provide enough money in the aggregate to bring the average incomes of the poorest 10 percent of the population up to the poverty-income threshold. However, they did bring the average incomes of the next poorest 10 percent over that threshold.[7]

---

7. Benjamin Bridges, Jr., *Redistributive Effects of Transfer Payments among Age and Economic Status Groups* (Washington, D.C.: U. S. Department of Health, Education, and Welfare, Social Security Administration, 1971).

But the programs are also very uneven in their incidence. They do a much better job of eliminating poverty among older families than among younger families, especially those with heads below forty-five years old, many with children: even after transfer payments, the incomes of the poorest nonaged families in the aggregate in 1966 were a little over half of what was needed to raise them to the poverty threshold. This is not surprising, because more than half of total income-maintenance payments were made to persons age sixty-five and over. Some people in poverty receive little or nothing from these programs; other people in poverty receive enough to lift them well above the poverty threshold; and substantial payments are made to people who were not in poverty prior to receipt of transfer payments. In fact, in 1966, more than 40 percent of all income-maintenance payments went to people who were not poor to begin with.

These facts do not necessarily condemn the programs, for while all are designed to make up for loss of income or inability to earn income, only the public-assistance program (and a few smaller programs) makes poverty a condition of payment. In most programs payments are related to prior earnings and may be made despite continued (although reduced) earnings, substantial savings, or a short-term drop in earnings (as in unemployment insurance). Although the present income-maintenance system does achieve a variety of worthwhile social goals, it is relatively ineffectual as a specific cure for poverty pure and simple.

Since 1939 social security payments have been made to the elderly retired and their survivors, and old-age assistance payments (part of "welfare") have been given to the indigent aged. Nevertheless, there were 2.2 million elderly persons below the poverty line in American metropolitan areas in 1971. Since the early 1950s, the social security program has provided benefits to disabled workers, and there is also a welfare program for indigent disabled persons. Nevertheless, in 1971 close to 1 million persons in urban areas were in poverty because of the disability of the male head of household. Since 1935 we have had a program of aid to dependent children designed to assist families in which the male parent is absent for one reason or another. Despite that, in 1971 there were 5.4 million persons in poverty in families headed by females in metropolitan areas.

Direct federal programs, such as social security, are uniform nationally, but very often involve low payments, and so individuals remain in poverty even though they receive benefits.[8] On the other hand, the public-assistance programs, such as aid to dependent children, vary tremendously among the states in coverage and in adequacy of payments. In several of the large urban states, families being given public assistance do receive enough to be above the officially defined poverty line. But in most of the South and in a good many other states as well, recipients of public assistance remain far below the poverty line.

One major criticism of the present public-assistance system is that the whole process is very degrading and involves a maximum amount of surveillance by public-assistance caseworkers. Usually, caseworkers are so busy investigating eligibility for payments that they have neither the time, inclination, nor the appropriate interpersonal relationships to permit them to do any real counseling or family guidance. This presumably is what social work schools train them to do. In contrast, in many other countries (like Britain), there is complete ad-

---

8. This will be less true in the future. Social security amendments in 1972 substantially increased benefit levels and provided for further automatic increases in future years.

ministrative separation of the income-maintenance system from the counseling and guidance services.

The present system of public assistance has also been criticized as providing a substantial deterrent to work efforts. Until quite recently, if a recipient earned any money, there was a dollar-for-dollar reduction in his or her assistance payments. Unless the principal wage earner could get a very good job indeed, one providing earnings well in excess of the public-assistance payments, there was no reason to make any effort to work. If the only available job was a part-time one or a low-wage one, that would not permit a family to get off assistance completely, going to work would not lead to a net improvement in the family's financial position. This has been referred to as a "100 percent tax" on earnings by recipients of public assistance.

These deficiencies in present income-maintenance programs —that is, the low levels of payments, the wide interstate disparities, the complex administrative procedures, and the work disincentives—are by now widely recognized. The rapid rise in welfare rolls since the early 1960s has brought home the failure of the system. Today both liberals and conservatives agree that there is a welfare crisis calling for fundamental reforms. Such reforms were advanced by liberal economists in the mid-1960s, were endorsed by a special commission appointed by President Johnson near the end of his term of office, and were formally recommended to the Congress by President Nixon in 1970. They have been debated in the Congress since then, but as of early 1973 were enacted only in part.

Three of the four major elements common to nearly all welfare reform proposals are now law. The first is the removal of what can only be described as a bizarre anomaly in our system—the subjection of large numbers of poor persons and households whom we presumably want to remove from poverty to the federal income tax. Tax legislation in 1969 effectively exempted everyone below the poverty threshold from the income tax, for the first time in at least fifteen years. Second, social security benefits were substantially raised in 1972. Third, the so-called adult public-assistance programs, covering the aged and the disabled, were federalized, thus raising payment levels substantially in many states. Together, the second and third elements of welfare reform should come close to removing from poverty those who are poor because of old age or disability.

The fourth element has been the most controversial. It deals with poverty among younger households whose head is not disabled, households headed by women or by men who are unemployed, intermittently employed, or employed at very low wages that do not sustain large families. President Nixon's proposal was the Family Assistance Plan (FAP), which is a variant of the so-called negative income tax.

The essential attribute of the negative income tax is that it is an income transfer system under which the payment from the government is reduced by a specified percentage as the family's other income rises. It thus offers more of a work incentive than the existing public assistance programs have traditionally done. It is called a negative income tax because it parallels our familiar positive income tax. Under the latter, families with income *above* a stated level make payments *to* the government and the payment rises as a fraction of income as income increases. Under the former, families with income *below* a stated level would receive payments *from* the government, the payment rising as a fraction of total income as income declines, until the payment reaches 100 percent of income at some low-level minimum guarantee. In the original version of President Nixon's proposal, the minimum guarantee for a family of four was $2,400, and such a family would be able to retain one-third of any income it earned. Thus, any family of four with earnings below $3,600 would receive some negative tax payment.

This is illustrated in Table 3-2. Families of four with incomes of less than $3,600 from sources other than FAP would receive some FAP payment. Families with incomes between $3,600 and $4,300 would receive no FAP payment and pay no income tax. Families with incomes above $4,300 pay income tax, which rises as a percentage of before- and after-tax income. There would be, therefore, a tax-and-transfer system that is symmetrical, with both positive and negative tax payments.

The proposal is highly controversial in part for ideological reasons, just as reform of the positive income tax involves ideological dispute: we disagree about just how much income redistribution government should engage in. But there is a genuine problem of "social engineering" or program design, as well, for it is difficult to reconcile even those objectives that all welfare reformers share. There is general agreement that the welfare system should assure some minimally adequate level of income, thus eliminating destitution (especially among children); that the system should encourage people to work; that it should be fair in treating equally needy people equally, no matter where they live or what the cause of their low income (other than an outright refusal to work); and that the total cost of the program must be kept within some bounds— it cannot be a large fraction of the gross national product. A high minimum guarantee endangers work incentives and raises program costs. Allowing people to keep a large fraction of their earnings encourages work incentives, but it raises program costs substantially and, besides, it would require payments to families that are by no means poor. For example,

TABLE 3-2 *Positive and Negative Income Taxes for Family of Four (Original Version of Family Assistance Plan and 1972 Income Tax Tables)*

Income from All Other Sources	Present Situation		Under Family Assistance Plan (FAP)		
	Income Tax Liability[a]	Net Income after Tax	FAP Payment[b]	Net Income after Tax and FAP Payment	Payment to (+) or from (−) Government as Percent of Net Income
0	0	0	$2,400	$2,400	−100
$ 1,000	0	$1,000	1,733	2,733	−63
2,000	0	2,000	1,067	3,067	−35
3,000	0	3,000	400	3,400	−12
3,600	0	3,600	0	3,600	0
4,000	0	4,000	0	4,000	0
5,000	$102	4,898	0	4,898	+2
6,000	249	5,751	0	5,751	+4
—					
10,000	901	9,099	0	9,099	+10

[a]From 1972 income tax tables, taxpayer with four exemptions not itemizing deductions.
[b]Minimum guarantee of $2,400 reduced by 66$\frac{2}{3}$ percent of other income.

if the guarantee is $2,400 and people are permitted to keep eighty cents out of every dollar earned, payments would be made up to earned incomes of $12,000. It would hardly seem fair to provide public assistance to $12,000-a-year families, while others have to subsist on $2,400.

Welfare reform is perhaps the most dramatic illustration of a common situation in public affairs today, especially in regard to policies concerning health, education, and welfare. The richest, most technically advanced country in the world has difficulty in solving its social problems not just because our priorities are wrong or because there are mean-spirited people among us, but more importantly because the solutions are genuinely difficult.[9]

The work incentives issue is one that has been, rightly, of special concern to economists. Many radicals, liberals and welfare professionals deplore the recent emphasis on "workfare rather than welfare," especially when it involves encouraging, if not compelling, low-income mothers to work. It seems inhumane, a hard-hat backlash. But there are humane reasons, as well as hard-hearted economic ones, to worry about work incentives. To begin with, the level of income support that *any* reformed welfare system is likely to provide will be quite low. Suppose the minimum guarantee for a family of four were set at $4,300, roughly the 1972 poverty-income threshold, rather than the $2,400 in the original version of FAP. While this would greatly increase program costs it would still provide only a bare subsistence level of income in urban areas. The Bureau of Labor Statistics annually prices cost-of-living budgets for families in American cities, at three different

---

9. Alice M. Rivlin of the Brookings Institution, a former assistant secretary of Health, Education, and Welfare, outlined this brilliantly in "Why Can't We Get Things Done?" *The Brookings Bulletin* 9, no. 2 (Spring 1972).

standards of living. Its lowest-level budget, which provides only a rather modest standard of living in metropolitan areas, cost more than $7,500 a year at prices prevailing in the spring of 1972, far above any conceivable income-maintenance level. It is therefore hardly humane *not* to encourage low-income people to try to do better than welfare, by working.

Second, work does confer status in our society, and a very large fraction of women of working age are in fact employed in nearly all advanced societies. It is no accident that the women's liberation movement has strongly urged measures that would help women at all economic levels to work.

Third, however rich the country may seem, our human and material resources are not equal to the demands we make on them: ours remains an economy of relative scarcity in which the opportunity costs of not using human resources to the fullest are very real. In this most important sense, we simply cannot afford to retain policies and institutions that act as a deterrent to useful employment. To be sure, we do not know precisely how great the work disincentives in various alternative income-maintenance programs are. However, we are in the process of learning a good deal more on this score. In a number of states and cities, large-scale controlled social experiments, financed by the federal government, are now being used to test the impact of income-maintenance alternatives. These are among the very first large-scale, scientific social experiments that have ever been undertaken. So far the results suggest that the negative income tax will have substantial positive effects on work incentives.[10]

Finally, a word on costs. It would not be terribly expensive to eliminate poverty in the sense of bringing all families in the

10. See David N. Kershaw, "A Negative-Income-Tax Experiment," *Scientific American,* October 1972.

country up to the Social Security Administration definition of poverty (which is a very conservative definition, to be sure). To achieve that in 1971 would have required an expansion of income-maintenance programs—and a concentration of the increased expenditure on those who were truly poor—by about $12 billion. This can be compared with the $75 billion or so actually spent in 1971 for the income-maintenance programs, much of which does not reach the very poorest families and individuals.

In 1971 personal disposable income after taxes totaled nearly $750 billion. This implies that if the richest 60 percent of all households in the country (those who account for 80 percent of total disposable income) were each to sacrifice 2 percent of their 1971 incomes (which compares to the average growth rate in family income, adjusted for price increases, of 3 percent annually since 1960), poverty could be eliminated in the sense that minimally adequate incomes could be supplied to all families in the United States.

Conclusion

Employment policies and income-maintenance policies are not mutually exclusive alternatives, although the organization of this chapter may have implied as much. Indeed, it seems likely that an adequate, properly designed system of income maintenance is a necessary precondition, if employment policies are to work at all. Consider, for example, one experience during the 1970–1971 recession. Most of the employment policies discussed in the earlier part of this chapter that have actually been adopted were begun in the booming conditions of the late 1960s. In most cases, they worked with limited efficacy and at high cost even then, and with the onset of the recession, even the limited success stories often turned into failure. This was particularly true of manpower-training programs: employers lost interest, it became difficult to place trainees, and recently graduated trainees were among the first to be laid off because they had the least seniority. Had a truly adequate income-maintenance system been available as a backstop, these recession-caused disappointments would have been much less demoralizing. Moreover, by helping to maintain the level of personal income in low-income neighborhoods an adequate income-support system would have provided a better prop for fledgling black capitalists and other efforts at ghetto economic development.

In one sense, and quite apart from the recession experience, employment policies in general must be regarded as less economically efficient than the expenditure of similar sums for a more generous income-maintenance system. To give low income people more cash to spend as they see fit will surely improve their immediate economic satisfaction more than spending the same amount of money on programs that involve expensive administration and costly new facilities. This follows from the basic value judgment (made in Chapter 1) that each person can appraise his own well-being better than can anyone else and thus is best off when he himself makes the decisions on how to use a given sum of money. Moreover, employment policies generally take much longer to be effective than does income maintenance. Programs with lengthy training and construction periods whose benefits are realized only over a period of years are very likely to have a less favorable ratio of benefits to costs, when these are properly discounted, than programs in which the timing of the expenditure and realization of the benefits coincide.

On the other hand, some of the employment policies discussed in this chapter are desirable for reasons other than the alleviation of poverty per se. For example, as we shall see in

Chapter 5, sensible policies for the use of land in metropolitan areas can improve access to jobs for the urban poor, and can confer other advantages as well. Appropriate transportation pricing will also help in this respect, and such pricing is badly needed, quite apart from the needs of the poor. Unreasonable prerequisites for jobs make no sense on any score. A considerable part of the need for training programs stems from the failures of a school system on which vast sums are now inefficiently spent. At the very minimum, money and resources that are going to be spent in urban areas in any case should be spent in ways that have at least a marginally beneficial effect on the poor. Employment policies of this type may well prove to be cases in which there are added benefits without any added costs.

In this chapter nothing has been said about the radical view of the urban poverty problem, the so-called "dual labor market" theory. This theory holds that the situation often prevailing in large cities in developing countries, particularly in Latin America, also applies in large American cities. In Latin American cities, people who hold regular jobs typically are reasonably well treated, because of trade union protection and social legislation; they receive decent wages and a variety of fringe benefits. Indeed, it is widely believed that the money costs of labor per unit of output frequently exceed the "shadow price" of labor, that is, its real resource costs in a well-functioning labor market. On the other hand, everyone else in these cities —often 30 percent or more of the potential labor force—is either unemployed or sporadically employed in fringe occupations, like lottery selling, with desperately low earnings.

The dual-market theorists maintain that unionization and the like have produced a similar situation here, dooming large numbers of people—particularly younger males in minority groups—to a lifetime of very low earnings outside the primary labor market. Although there are good reasons to doubt the validity of the theory (including substantial empirical evidence that considerable occupational upgrading does occur among minority groups) it is worth saying a few words about the policy implications of the theory, if it is valid. The most obvious such implication, drawn by the radical theorists, is the pressing need for a comprehensive reformation of the entire social and economic system, that is, the demise of capitalism. Because capitalism strikes at least 90 percent of the American people as a smashing economic success, its early demise is, at best, unlikely. What then?

The existence of a permanent and untractable dual labor market should logically call for emphasis on generous income-maintenance policies, with little, if any, concern for work incentives. If the only available work is intermittent, menial, and low paid, we would have to accept the fact that large numbers of people in our cities must be supported by income payments from government that have no connection with work at all. Employment policies of the type discussed in this chapter would have no relevance for the poverty problems, and the money committed to them should be diverted to income support systems not connected with work. Such arrangements, if implemented, would surely confirm the theorists in time, because we soon would truly have two societies in our cities, with differing and antagonistic life styles and mores. It is a fair presumption, however, that the two societies would also differ greatly in economic well-being, with a relatively rich working population providing the most grudging of income support to the rest. It is no doubt not for the economist to say, but this does seem a recipe for repression, not revolution.

4

Housing Markets and
Housing Policies

In Chapter 2, we isolated three types of continuing urban housing problems: the low quality of the housing
available to many poor families, particularly among the racial
minorities in central cities; the vast areas of aging and stag-
nating neighborhoods surrounding the out-and-out slums in
the larger and older American cities; and the limited range of
choice among combinations of price, accessibility, and amenity
confronting all but the richest families in the larger metropolitan areas.

Awareness of these problems is not new, although they have
often been described in rather different terms. Congress began enacting laws designed to solve them more than twenty
years ago. The housing conditions of the poor were to be improved by building a great amount of low-rent public housing,
with heavy subsidization by the federal government. The gray
areas were to be rebuilt and rehabilitated under urban renewal
programs, also with substantial federal subsidy. And the housing choice of the entire population was to be expanded, by
making mortgage credit cheaper and mortgage terms (down
payments and length of the repayment period) easier for both

single-family houses and apartments, thus putting new housing within the reach of lower-middle-income as well as upper-middle-income families.

All of these things have been done to some extent, but these actions have come nowhere near solving the problems. The Housing Act of 1949, the landmark legislation, set as its goal: "Realization as soon as feasible . . . of a decent home and a suitable living environment for every American family." But more recently, in enacting the Housing and Urban Development Act of 1968, Congress declared that the 1949 goal had not been realized for the poor. It reaffirmed the goal and specified the quantitative dimensions of the measures needed to reach the goal: the construction or rehabilitation of 26 million housing units over the next decade, 6 million for low- and moderate-income families. This means an annual rate of housing production nearly double that of the 1950s and 1960s and a tenfold increase in the annual output of subsidized housing for low- and middle-income families during those years.

Housing the Urban Poor

Clearly, the policies used in the past must have been inadequate or inappropriate, especially for low-income urban families. Postmortems on past policies are seldom interesting or useful, but it is worthwhile considering whether past as well as present policies may not involve a fundamental error.

In nearly all American cities, building and housing codes define the physical characteristics of the lowest-quality housing units that it is permissible to build. Construction technology, work practices and wage rates, land prices, building materials costs, and interest rates determine the prices at which such minimum-quality housing units must sell or rent. It turns out, of course, that these prices are higher than can be afforded by families in the lower half of the income distribution. As has been pointed out:

> . . . the income which any household must attain to rent or buy adequate quality housing without spending too high a proportion of its total income on housing is significantly higher than the official "poverty level" as defined by the Social Security Administration, which is based on costs of an adequate diet rather than on costs of adequate housing. There are millions more "housing poor" households in the United States than "food poor" households.[1]

This, too, is not a recent development. Lower-income families seldom have been able to afford *new* unsubsidized housing in cities. Instead, they occupy older housing that is less attractive to its earlier occupants and therefore commands lower prices or rents. But the prices or rents for older housing units are too high for the urban poor, unless the housing units are grossly overcrowded by poor families or unless the old housing has greatly deteriorated physically. Here, too, building and housing codes and the community's determination of acceptable minimum housing standards are at work: we are unwilling, as a nation and as individual cities, to tolerate gross overcrowding and physical deterioration.

The set of housing policies prevalent in the United States works on the cost side of the imbalance between the costs of minimum-standard housing and the income necessary to pay for these costs. We subsidize rents in public housing; we subsidize land costs; we provide interest rates on mortgages far below the market; and we worry about means to reduce actual

---

1. Anthony Downs, "Moving Toward Realistic Housing Goals," in *Agenda for the Nation,* ed. Kermit Gordon (Washington, D.C.: The Brookings Institution, 1968), p. 147.

construction costs. A wholly different approach would be to concern ourselves largely with the income side: raise incomes of the urban poor by the various means discussed in Chapter 3, and let the private housing industry satisfy the greatly expanded effective demand for housing. Clearly, this would be much easier administratively, for a wide range of governmental housing programs could be dismantled, but would it work?

The conventional wisdom regarding the demand for housing suggests that it might not. For many years, observers have cited statistics that seem to show that as income rises a smaller percentage of that income is spent on housing—that is, the income elasticity of demand for housing is low. This implies that if the incomes of low-income families were substantially raised, they would spend smaller percentages of their incomes for housing, and therefore they would not buy housing services that are as much better in quality as their new, higher incomes would permit. That is, they would spend more for other consumer products, but very little extra for housing. If this occurred, it surely would not stimulate the private housing industry to greatly expand the supply of housing for the poor or, indeed, for anyone else.

If the residents of a city or metropolitan area or the nation as a whole are arrayed by income and housing expenditures at a given moment, the income elasticity of demand for housing does indeed appear to be very low. For example, evidence from the 1960 Census of Housing for the metropolitan counties of northeastern New Jersey shows that the average value of the housing units occupied by families with incomes between $5,000 and $7,000 was less than 20 percent greater than that occupied by families with incomes only half as high.[2]

---

2. Dick Netzer, *Economics of the Property Tax* (Washington, D.C.: The Brookings Institution, 1966), p. 291.

Nationwide surveys of consumer finance in the late 1960s similarly show that the median value of houses owned by families with incomes around the national average is less than one-third greater than the value of houses owned by families with incomes just above the poverty line, incomes that are less than half the national average. Data of this type suggest that the income elasticity of demand for housing of poor families may be below 0.3; that is, a 10 percent increase in income may elicit less than a 3 percent rise in housing expenditure.

However, this kind of evidence has been vigorously challenged in recent years. The main criticism is that such evidence, by taking a snapshot as of a given moment, ignores the characteristic life cycle of families as housing consumers, as well as their actual decision-making processes. In reality, people make housing decisions on the basis of the incomes they expect over some longer period of time, rather than on the basis of the income actually received in a given year. Thus, many of the elderly poor live in housing they acquired years earlier, when their incomes were much higher; many people who have just recently managed to emerge from poverty have not yet arranged to relocate in better housing that would be more appropriate to the change in their long-term income expectations. Studies that have been made of "permanent" or lifetime incomes and housing expenditures suggest strongly that the percentage of permanent income devoted to housing does not decline significantly as permanent income rises and may actually increase.

For example, in the study of northeastern New Jersey cited previously, estimates were made of the expected average annual lifetime incomes of people in various occupational groups (because income prospects are closely related to occupation). It was found that the average value of the housing units occupied by the various occupational groups closely reflected the differences in expected lifetime incomes.[3] Other studies have found income elasticities for renters, with respect to permanent income, of just below 1.0 (that is, expenditures for rent and income increase proportionately) and elasticities for homeowners of well above 1.0.[4]

Because housing decisions tend to be made on a long-term basis, any snapshot evidence cannot take adequate account of important economic events that are occurring over time that will strongly influence housing decisions. During the first half of the twentieth century, the nation as a whole most certainly did not increase its expenditure for housing in proportion to the very large increases in its income. The per capita value of housing, expressed in dollars of constant purchasing power, was only slightly higher in 1950 than it was in 1890.[5] During this same period, national income per capita, in constant dollars, tripled. Comparable estimates for periods between 1930 and 1970 appear in Table 4-1. They show that although the per capita real value of the housing stock actually declined between 1930 and 1950, at a time when per capita real GNP was rising significantly, more recent trends have differed sharply: the value of the housing stock actually increased slightly more than GNP in the 1950s; in the 1960s, the older pattern of apparent income inelasticity reappeared, but housing performance was far better relative to GNP than in the period from 1890 to 1950.

How can this be explained? There were powerful forces at work, quite aside from changes in average incomes. During

---

3. Netzer, *Economics of the Property Tax,* p. 296 and fig. 6, p. 64.
4. See Frank deLeeuw, "The Demand for Housing: A Review of Cross-Sectional Evidence," *The Review of Economics and Statistics* 58 (February 1971).
5. Leo Grebler, David M. Blank, and Louis Winnick, *Capital Formation in Residential Real Estate* (Princeton, N. J.: Princeton University Press, 1956), pp. 252–260.

the 1930s, the collapse of many financial institutions and mass unemployment severely restricted new housing construction, and virtually no housing was built during World War II. Another important variable was the change in the price of housing relative to other goods and services. Fragmentary evidence suggests that construction costs were increasing at a higher

TABLE 4-1 *The U.S. Housing Stock and GNP, 1930-1970*

| | Percent Change during Period | | |
	1930-1950	1950-1960	1960-1970
Per Capita Value, in Constant Dollars, of Nonfarm Housing Stock at Year End	−15	+18	+11
Per Capita Gross National Product, in Constant Dollars	+58	+16	+30

Source: Housing-stock data adapted from estimates in *Survey of Current Business*, November 1971. They apply to net stocks (after depreciation) of nonfarm housekeeping units, divided by the nonfarm population living in households (rather than in "group quarters").

rate than other prices in the early part of the century. Much better data show that, during the 1950s, construction costs rose more slowly than other prices, while they rose more rapidly than other prices in the 1960s. It is logical to suppose that these price changes may explain much of the apparent long-term inelasticity of housing expenditure with respect to income: when housing is a good buy relative to other things, families do spend the additional amounts for housing that their rising incomes permit.

If the demand for housing today is in fact reasonably sensitive to income, people will abandon low-quality housing and slum neighborhoods as they become better off. This would seem to argue that income transfers would be as efficacious as housing subsidies in improving the housing conditions of the poor. But there are some further difficulties in the income-transfer strategy.

One is a short-term difficulty. If the incomes of the central-city poor were rapidly increased, the immediate effect would be a sharp rise in the price of the existing housing stock. Few central cities have any supply of unoccupied decent housing into which people could move when their higher incomes permitted them to pay higher rents or prices. More generally, the addition to the supply of housing that can be provided by the construction industry within a short period is only a small fraction of the existing housing supply. If 5 million poor families suddenly had the income to command better housing, house prices and rents would rise sharply during the three, four, or more years it would take, under the most favorable conditions, to expand the nation's housing stock by 5 million units above and beyond that necessary to accommodate the normal increase in new families being formed. Because central cities have relatively little vacant land on which to build and because the minority-group poor are concentrated there, the price and rent increases would be especially severe in the central cities.

In addition, the income-transfer strategy may not help in changing the character of whole neighborhoods. Our national housing policy is not concerned solely with the physical characteristics of an individual housing unit, but more generally with the quality of the physical environment in which children in poor families grow up: the housing unit itself, the building, the block, and the neighborhood. This larger environment cannot be transformed by improving a single building in a slum neighborhood.

Moreover, it is doubtful whether it is really sensible to expect that greatly increased incomes will result in improvement or replacement of individual buildings. Both the individual households that might buy housing units (using their higher incomes) and the investors that might be attracted by increased housing demand are unlikely to put much money into scattered buildings in a generally squalid neighborhood, particularly one that seems on its way to becoming a "zone of destruction" (see Chapter 2). The ownership of slum housing typically is highly fragmented, and therefore the potential investor in private housing does confront exactly this situation. Thus, the response to a pure income-transfer strategy is likely to be an effort to leave the old neighborhoods, rather than their reconstruction under private auspices. Indeed, this seems to be precisely what has been happening in the zones of destruction. Conceivably, a sudden large increase in housing demand could change the investment outlook of the many small-scale owners of rental housing in inner-city areas and make them hopeful once again, but this is unlikely to happen unless such owners also have access to adequate financing and managerial skills and can expect the neighborhoods to be free from devastating violent crime, vandalism, and racial conflict.

In short, a housing strategy, as well as an income strategy, seems essential if the housing problems of the urban poor are to be attacked successfully. That strategy must assure sufficient increases in the total supply of decent housing, so that higher incomes are not dissipated in higher prices with little improvement in quality. It must also include governmental action to deal with the needed upgrading of whole neighborhoods. Public intervention usually means subsidy, in direct money terms or indirectly in the form of lowered interest rates, the use of public powers to condemn property, and the mobilization and application of managerial energy and administrative talent, which well may be the single most important factor.

Housing Supply and Cost Policies

During the twentieth century, but especially in the past twenty-five years, American governments—federal, state, and local—have equipped themselves with a large number of policy tools designed to increase the accessible supply of good-quality housing, either in general or for selected income groups, by lowering the price at which housing is offered to consumers or by offering special incentives for public or private builders of housing. In addition, they have adopted a number of policies not specifically designed to affect housing supply and costs, but which nonetheless do so, some for better and some for worse. These policies can be grouped into five main classes, according to their principal effects:

1. Subsidizing the initial outlay for land and/or construction of housing.
2. Making mortgage credit cheaper and/or more readily available.
3. Changing factors that affect the costs of construction and land and, thereby, the price at which a newly completed, unsubsidized housing unit can be sold or rented.
4. Affecting the tax burdens borne by housing occupants and investors in housing.
5. Changing the decision-making powers of private owners by controlling rents, directly affecting maintenance and repair decisions (for example, through enforcement of housing codes), or restructuring ownership (for example, conversion to cooperative ownership of rental housing even for families with modest incomes).

DIRECT SUBSIDIES FOR CAPITAL OUTLAY

During the 1930s New Deal housing reformers sought to improve the housing conditions of the poor by the obvious and direct means then widely used in other industrial countries in Europe—government construction and management of multifamily housing projects to be occupied by low-income families at heavily subsidized rents. Because local and state governments had extremely limited tax-raising capabilities during the Great Depression, the U.S. Housing Act of 1937 provided for federal subsidies; by 1950, 202,000 housing units had been constructed under that and similar federal legislation. The Magna Carta of American housing legislation, the Housing Act of 1949, provided for a greatly expanded federal low-rent housing program, envisaging the construction of 800,000 units over a six-year period.

The subsidy mechanism was a simple one. Local public authorities were to be formed. They would issue bonds to raise the funds needed for the new housing, and the federal government would make annual subsidy payments to the local governments to cover the interest and bond repayment obligations. Rents collected from tenants would pay the operating costs, and these rents would be scaled to the incomes of the tenants. Because the subsidy was so substantial,[6] severe income limits were imposed to assure that only the truly poor benefited from the subsidy.

---

6. For example, in 1967, the 62,000 families living in federally subsidized public housing in New York City paid an average monthly rent of $64, toward operating expenses averaging $70; in addition, there was a federal debt-service subsidy of $49 per month per apartment. David Dreyfuss and Joan Hendrickson, *A Guide to Government Activities in New York City's Housing Markets* (The RAND Corporation, Memorandum RM-5673-NYC, November 1968), p. 18.

The program has moved far more slowly than had been anticipated. The six-year goal posted in 1949 was not reached until 1973, twenty-four years later, when a total of roughly a million federally subsidized units (including those built under the 1930s legislation) were in operation.[7] In part, this has been because of congressional reluctance to appropriate funds for the program. In most years, Congress has authorized subsidies for no more than 35,000 new units. But there are other reasons as well, reasons that partly explain the congressional unwillingness to carry through on the 1949 commitment.

The most important of these reasons are connected with the problem of finding sites for public housing projects. The available vacant sites for any kind of housing tend to be in the outer parts of central cities and, still more, in suburban areas. But residents of middle-income neighborhoods usually oppose the construction of low-income housing in their midst and central-city housing authorities have no power to construct housing in suburbs (unlike their counterparts in Britain and some other countries). This difficulty has existed from the beginning of the public housing program, but has become worse as blacks and other racial minority groups have come to make up a larger and larger proportion of the central-city poor with incomes low enough to qualify for public housing.

The alternative is to build public housing in the existing slum or ghetto areas, a strategy with two major disadvantages. First, the ghetto areas usually have high population densities and little vacant land (except in the form of small scattered sites where demolished houses once stood), so that acquiring

---

7. A few states and cities have supplementary subsidized low-rent public housing programs; they involve fewer than 100,000 units, largely in New York State. New York City accounts for 54,000 of these units, most of which have state debt-service subsidies similar to the federal subsidies. Dreyfuss and Hendrickson, *New York City's Housing Markets,* pp. 19–24.

sites often means the displacement of many low-income families. Second, this strategy strengthens income and racial segregation, which central-city governments usually wish to avoid. The result is that the program is slowed, while housing authorities try to find sites outside the ghettos and attempt to overcome neighborhood opposition to use of these sites for public housing.

The difficulty in finding sites encourages housing authorities to build as many units as possible on each site, in the form of high-rise buidings. This, however, leads to high construction costs, because high-rise buidings cost far more per housing unit than do garden apartments or row houses. Congress, in an effort to limit the federal government's fiscal liabilities, has included cost ceilings in the public housing legislation, and in the larger cities, public housing authorities continually bump up against these ceilings.

Until quite recently, the one thing that did work in the public housing program was its financing scheme, under which the capital costs were federally subsidized, but rents paid for operating costs, including payments to local governments in lieu of property taxes. Housing authorities generally have had high maintenance standards, which is appropriate for the costly high-rise buildings characteristic of public housing in large cities. Rapidly rising labor costs in the late 1960s pushed operating costs above rental income in many places. To increase rents sufficiently to eliminate operating deficits would have forced out many of the tenants who were not on public assistance, and would have thus changed the nature of the target population. Congress intervened to prevent this and, for the first time, provided operating subsidies in addition to the debt-service subsidies. Although the housing authorities claim that the operating subsidies are inadequate and that they will therefore be threatened with bankruptcy sooner or later, a parsimonious federal attitude is understandable, because the operating subsidies could increase without limit. The problem is essentially an insoluble one, if operating costs continue to increase more rapidly than the incomes of the working poor for whom public housing was originally intended.

A program involving heavy subsidies, conflict over site selection, and overtones of racial segregation is bound to be unpopular in Congress and in individual cities. In addition, public housing was, to some extent, oversold in its early days. Housing reformers somehow managed to convey the impression that subsidized low-rent housing would ameliorate all sorts of social problems in the slums, above and beyond simply improving the housing conditions of the poor. This has clearly not been the case; many hold public housing in bad repute merely because it has not achieved social objectives it never was capable of achieving.

The Housing Act of 1949 included another form of direct subsidy of the capital cost of housing. Title I of that act provided subsidies for assembly of land in blighted areas for urban renewal. Under Title I, local governments buy and clear land in blighted areas and then transfer it to private developers (or public agencies, like housing authorities) at a much lower cost. The federal government makes grants to cover most of the differences between the costs of buying the land, relocating the occupants, and razing the building and the resale price. It thus subsidizes the land component of the capital costs of the new uses of the sites. Typically, the land is resold for one-fourth of what it cost to acquire and clear, and the federal government provides two-thirds of the loss or "write-down" of land values involved in a project.

Although the rhetoric of urban renewal and slum clearance has been associated with the notion of improving urban housing conditions and although the write-down has been a direct subsidy, urban renewal is really not designed primarily to increase the supply of housing. The main goal is to improve neighborhoods in cities, by making a complete change in land use in the project areas. This often involves a *reduction* in housing supply, and on balance the program has removed more units from the nation's housing stock than it has replaced. In many cases, this is because blighted residential areas are converted to new commercial or industrial uses. When all the projects under way between 1949 and 1966 are completed, 42,000 acres (net of streets) will have been cleared and redeveloped, but only 20,000 acres will be devoted to residential uses. In many projects that are largely residential, high-density blighted housing is replaced by better, but fewer, new housing units.

The negative effect of urban renewal on the gross supply of housing is especially marked for the low-income population. Few urban renewal projects include new, low-rent housing units. But most of the sites, before renewal, have been occupied by low-income families in low-quality (but low-rent) housing. Between 1949 and 1966, nearly 1,200 projects in more than 800 cities had been started (over 250 of these were completed). Well over 80 percent of the 450,000 housing units originally on these sites were substandard, that is, physically dilapidated or lacking full plumbing facilities. Over 95 percent of the families in this housing had incomes low enough to qualify them for public housing; most of these were black or in the Spanish minorities. Only a minority of these low-income families actually were rehoused in public housing, because the public housing program has fallen so far short of its quantitative goals. It is therefore not surprising that, just as public housing is unpopular among the nonpoor white majority in urban America, urban renewal is highly unpopular among the poor minorities.

MAKING CREDIT CHEAPER AND MORE AVAILABLE

Policies that operate through mortgage credit terms and availability have been by far the most popular of American housing strategies. They are popular with legislators, perhaps because the subsidy involved is disguised and, once the mortgage credit is offered, the decisions are made by private parties rather than public agencies, like housing authorities and urban renewal agencies. They are popular with voters, perhaps because nearly everyone in the country, not just the poor, is a potential beneficiary of one or another of the various mortgage credit policies.

Three main types of mortgage credit policies have been used. The first, the oldest, and most widely applicable has been to provide federal government guarantees or insurance of individual mortgages written on far more generous terms than had been conventional in earlier years. The government guarantee or insurance, by reducing the risk and standardizing the provisions of the mortgage loan, converted mortgages into national credit market instruments and attracted new types of lenders into the mortgage market. For example, it made it feasible for eastern financial institutions to invest surplus funds in home mortgages in rapidly growing California. The increased geographic mobility of capital and the expansion of the whole pool of mortgage funds was a significant contribution to home building in the decade following World War II.

From the consumer's standpoint, the more generous terms have been even more important. In the 1920s, required down payments were usually half or more of the purchase price; mortgages ran for five years and had to be refinanced at the end of that time, which could not always be done. Under the government programs, down payments have been 10 percent of the purchase price, and sometimes even less; mortgages run for twenty years or longer, with constant monthly payments covering both interest and principal repayment. Families with little cash savings but good long-term income prospects thus found the home-buying market opened to them.

TABLE 4-2   *Extent of Government Mortgage Insurance Coverage in Metropolitan Areas, 1971 (Millions of Properties or Housing Units)*

	Homeowner and Rental Properties with 1-4 Units	Multifamily Rental Housing Units in Properties with 5 or More Units
Total Number inside Metropolitan Areas	28.1	9.1
In Properties Having Some Mortgage Debt	17.6	7.5
In Properties with FHA or VA Mortgages	7.7	0.6

Source: Adapted from *U.S. Census of Housing: 1970,* vol. 5, *Residential Finance* (1973). Excludes all publicly owned housing.

Government insurance of mortgages began with the establishment of the Federal Housing Administration (FHA) in 1934, in response to the financial crisis and virtual drying up of mortgage credit in the 1930s. Successive "GI Bills" provided for guarantees of mortgages obtained by veterans, usually on even more generous terms. By 1971, 43 percent of the mortgaged properties with four units or less in metropolitan areas had FHA or Veterans Administration (VA) mortgages; about 8 percent of the housing units in apartment houses with mortgages were covered by FHA rental-housing mortgage programs (see Table 4-2). For various reasons, including interest-rate ceilings, cost limitations, and just plain red tape, "conventional" mortgages made by local financial institutions like savings and loan associations dominate the mortgage

market. But under the influence of the FHA and VA programs, these conventional mortgages are nothing like their
counterparts of forty years ago. Like the FHA and VA mortgages, conventional mortgages too have relatively low down
payments and long repayment periods.

The standard mortgage insurance and guarantee programs
never were of much help to families in the lower half of the
income distribution. For example, the median new house
bought with an FHA thirty-year mortgage in 1971, valued
at just under $24,000, had estimated annual housing costs,
including taxes, insurance, heating, and upkeep, of more than
$3,500, implying the need for a family income in excess of
$14,000, well above the median family income of $11,000
in metropolitan areas in the United States in 1971. In most
urban areas, few families with incomes below $10,000 now
can afford to buy single-family houses.

A second type of mortgage credit policy has been developed
to offset rising interest rates and to reach lower into the income
distribution. This has taken the form of public borrowing, at
the lower interest rates that governments can command, and
relending the funds at these lower interest rates to individual
borrowers and builders. Governments can borrow at lower
rates because they are obviously better credit risks than individuals; moreover, interest on state and local government
bonds is exempt from federal income taxation and, therefore,
state-local obligations bear especially low interest rates.

The federal government began using this approach almost
as soon as the FHA began operations. It set up the Federal
National Mortgage Association (FNMA) to raise funds in the
capital market that could be used to buy FHA (and VA)
mortgages from lenders. When market interest rates rose, FHA
mortgages could, in effect, continue to be made at below-
market rates, because FNMA would buy them, and FNMA

needed only to get interest rates sufficient to cover the interest costs on its own obligations, costs that were lower than the rates on ordinary private mortgages. Since World War II, a number of states and cities have set up programs under which they borrow and relend to individuals for housing at preferential interest rates. Initially, these programs were for veterans. The largest of the veterans' programs (in California) has involved interest rates about two percentage points below the market rate on equivalent home loans.[8] Similar reductions in interest cost are characteristic of the newer state-local programs designed specifically for middle-income families.

The prototype of these is New York's Mitchell-Lama program, established in 1955. Under this program, state and city bonds are used to provide mortgages of as much as 100 percent of the capital costs of rental and cooperative apartment housing, for terms up to fifty years, at interest rates related to state and city borrowing costs. The developers are limited in their profits (they are most often nonprofit organizations); the occupants are subject to income limits, usually seven times the monthly costs. Together with property tax exemption, the interest advantage and profit limitations have permitted new housing to be offered at rents at least 40 percent below the unsubsidized private market. Originally, the program was aimed at families in the $6,000–$10,000 income range; with rising interest rates, construction and operating costs, the target population for new projects now is much higher, the $15,000–$25,000 income range.

Although such programs do not involve cash subsidies, the savings to consumers and the indirect costs to governments are significant. A two-percentage-point interest advantage will

---

8. The California program started in 1921, but was modest in size until after World War II.

save nearly $250 per $1,000 of mortgage amount over twenty years and more than $800 over fifty years. On a typical apartment under a fifty-year loan, this amounts to a reduction in rent of nearly $30 a month.

The indirect costs to governments reflect the fact that an increased volume of borrowing will raise the interest rates that government must pay on all its bonds. It is a simple demand-and-supply phenomenon—the issuance of housing bonds adds to the public sector's demand for capital, but has no impact on the supply of loanable funds. Therefore, the price a government pays for capital, the interest rate, will rise. Thus, by aiding housing in this form, governments make it more costly to provide the schools, roads, hospitals, and other facilities for which they are responsible. The policy may be desirable, on balance, but its costs should not be ignored, for housing is only one among a wide range of public goals.

The third credit policy is an extension of the second: to provide mortgage credit at rates so low that actual cash subsidies are required, that is, at interest rates below those a government must pay on its own bonds. In 1959 and 1961, Congress enacted two special low-interest, low-term loan programs aimed at providing housing for families with incomes just above the limits for eligibility for public housing. Initially, the interest rates were the same as those on outstanding federal debt, but because interest rates were rising, the rate for the programs was set at 3 percent in 1965.

The Housing Act of 1968 took another step to lower housing costs to occupants, thus lowering the target income level, by subsidizing interest costs. Sections 235 and 236 of the act (the former for homeowners, the latter for rental housing) provide for federal subsidies that, at a maximum, reduce the interest cost to the equivalent of a 1 percent mortgage. Tenants pay rents equal to 25 percent of income and homeowners make mortgage payments equal to 20 percent of income.[9] The federal subsidy makes up the difference between the amounts required by the actual mortgage on the new housing and the rents so established, subject to the maximum expressed in terms of a 1 percent interest rate. There are income limits, which together with the ceiling on the subsidies (typically, the ceiling will be on the order of $50–$60 a month per unit) mean that the programs are aimed at the $4,000–$7,000 income range.

TABLE 4-3   *Rentals and Family Income under Different Federal Housing Programs, for New Two-Bedroom Apartments*

Program	Monthly Rental	Annual Family Income If Rent Is No More Than 25 Percent of Income
Ordinary FHA Mortgage (No Subsidy—Section 207), Average	$227	$10,876
Below-Market-Interest-Rate Program (Section 221.d.3), Average	166	7,972
1-Percent-Interest-Rate Program (Section 236), Minimum	147	7,052
Public Housing, Average	97	4,644

Source: From The President's Committee on Urban Housing, *A Decent Home* (Final Report, December 1968), Table 2-2. The calculations apply to Detroit in 1967 and assume capital costs of about $17,000 per apartment. Costs are higher than this in the other very large cities, but Detroit is representative of the moderately large and medium-sized cities.

Table 4-3, based on data for Detroit in 1967, illustrates the effects of this for typical two-bedroom apartments. An apartment financed by an ordinary, market-interest-rate FHA

---

9. The lower figure for homeowners was set because they bear utility charges and maintenance and repair costs that are included in rents.

mortgage would have rented for $227 a month. If rent is to absorb no more than 25 percent of family income, the family must earn nearly $11,000 a year. At the other end of the spectrum, in heavily subsidized public housing, rents for such apartments averaged $97 a month in 1967, permitting a family income of $4,600, at a 25 percent rent-to-income ratio.

Even an extreme low-interest policy cannot reach people at the very bottom of the income scale, although efforts to improve the housing conditions of those just above the bottom are important. Moreover, these programs are the first ones in our history to be aimed at expanding the supply of housing for the near-poor, who have often been the most harshly affected by compulsory relocation when land is acquired for urban renewal, highways, public housing, and other public construction. Perhaps the most important innovation in these programs is the extension of the subsidy to homeowners. This will make little difference in the large central cities, but it could permit extensive building of homes for the near-poor in outlying areas, making possible significant steps toward achieving racial balance in American metropolitan areas.

The 1968 below-market-interest-rate programs have proved spectacularly successful, in one very important respect: a very large number of housing units have been built or purchased under the programs by families in the target income group. The programs have been beset by scandals in some places, with poorly constructed houses being sold to unsuspecting buyers whose incomes are too low to allow any real margin for unexpected repair costs. Together with layoffs in the 1970–1971 recession, this has led to much higher mortgage default rate than has been customary in FHA experience. The scandals and defaults in the Section 235 and 236 programs, the many problems with public housing, and the failure of urban renewal considered as a housing program have convinced some, including federal officials, that direct federal subsidies for new housing construction have been a failure on balance. They assert that these should be abandoned in favor of unrestricted federal grants to cities and states for community development and housing allowances—a form of income transfer—to individual families (housing allowances are discussed in a later section of this chapter). Other observers view the troubles with Section 235 and 236 as correctable "teething" difficulties and maintain that the programs are in fact doing just what they were designed to do—to quickly produce large amounts of housing for families with modest incomes.

It should be noted that most federal and state-local government mortgage credit programs apply to rehabilitation of existing housing as well as to new housing. Critics of American housing policy frequently point out the advantages of rehabilitation: the preservation of existing neighborhood social ties; the lesser need for relocation of existing occupants; the more human scale of existing buildings compared to the high-rise apartments that might otherwise replace them; the intrinsic architectural merits of some of the old neighborhoods.

But offsetting this are two major disadvantages. First, some of the old housing in the older cities is truly a "sow's ear." Even after rehabilitation, rooms are small, layout bad and access to light and air poor. Often, maintenance costs on the rehabilitated housing will be very high indeed, if it is not to sink back into slum status. Second, the costs of rehabilitation tend to be very high. Few economies of scale can be realized, because each building presents unique problems. The work tends to be highly labor-intensive and therefore prone to rapid increases in cost over time. Experience under rehabilitation programs is full of examples in which the rehabilitation costs were almost as high as those of building new housing units; on the basis of costs per square foot of living space, this is usually the case.

Rehabilitation, then, is a situation in which a variety of social benefits (plus the fact that rehabilitation often can be finished more quickly than new housing) must be compared to the high economic costs of a relatively low-quality finished product. Often, the balance will be on the side of an aggressive rehabilitation policy, but it is highly unlikely that a policy of rehabilitation *instead of* substantial new housing construction is the best one in any metropolitan area. For the inner city, however, rehabilitation and adequate maintenance of existing sound housing may be the sole option available.

POLICIES AFFECTING CONSTRUCTION AND LAND COSTS

It is obvious that outright reductions in the resource costs of providing additional housing units or improved housing quality are preferable, on economic or any other grounds, to subsidy. Moreover, it has seemed to most observers that there *must* be room for substantial cost savings, because productivity in construction has improved more slowly than productivity in the rest of private industry.[10] The reasons for this have been frequently discussed: the absence of mass production techniques; restrictive labor practices; and small-scale, noninnovative management are those most often mentioned.

Countless studies and commission reports have urged attention to construction cost-saving methods and have urged more research along these lines. Yet little has been accomplished. Perhaps one explanation lies in the small difference that any

10. Productivity is measured here as the increase in real national income originating in the industry per person engaged in production in that industry, 1950 to 1971.

single cost-saving technique can make in the final price at which housing is offered. Another is that construction costs in total are by no means the only determinant of the final price.

The President's Commission on Urban Housing, reporting in 1968, found that on-site labor costs typically account for only about 20 percent of initial development and construction costs. Materials account for another 35–40 percent; the remaining 35–40 percent is accounted for by land costs, overhead and profit, architects' fees, and the like. The initial capital costs in turn, when reflected in mortgage payments, account for only about 50 percent of monthly occupancy costs to the consumer, the rest being made up of taxes, utilities, maintenance, repairs, and so on.[11] Thus, even if very large construction cost savings were achieved—say, a reduction of one-fourth in materials costs and one-third in on-site labor costs—monthly housing costs to consumers would decline by less than 10 percent. This commission strongly urged new efforts to achieve the cost savings, but concluded that cost saving could not play a major part in a national housing strategy.

A few months later, the National Commission on Urban Problems, established to study the impact of building codes, zoning, and taxes on housing, reported a quite different conclusion. This commission argued that:

> No opportunity to reduce costs should be ignored simply because, by itself, it may not result in dramatic overall reductions in costs. . . . Housing costs can be reduced if none of the many avenues for savings is dismissed as inconsequential. Add them all up and they promise to be substantial.[12]

---

11. The President's Commission on Urban Housing, *A Decent Home* (Final Report, December 1968), pp. 10–11.
12. National Commission on Urban Problems, *Building the American City* (Final Report, 1969).

The commission pointed out, moreover, that property taxes, builders' markups, architects' fees, and numerous other costs are keyed to the original investment in labor and materials, so that the hypothetical cost reductions noted in the previous paragraph could easily result in an overall reduction in costs to consumers of 15 percent or more, which is hardly to be disregarded.

This disagreement between the two commissions illustrates a recurrent theme in discussions of public policy: the frequent tendency to take either-or positions. *Either* the policy under consideration by itself makes a dramatic impact, *or* it is not worth talking about. To economists, most economic phenomena are continuous functions; the question is whether the impact of policy A is more or less than that of policy B, rather than all or nothing. Construction costs surely can be reduced through public policy to some degree and therefore should be pursued, unless there are serious disadvantages to such policies.

One important consideration here is that governments, at the local level mainly, now pursue policies that serve to *raise* building and land costs. An obvious route toward reduction in costs is to revise such policies—zoning and similar land-use controls (especially in outlying areas) and building and housing codes. It should be obvious that any governmental intervention that limits the ways in which land can be used is likely to have the effect of raising land costs to developers. If some tracts of land cannot be legally used for some purposes or in specified ways, then the supply of land available for those purposes has been effectively reduced, and its price will rise.

This cost increase may be a necessary consequence of actions taken to secure other benefits. Zoning was introduced fifty years ago for entirely worthwhile purposes: to ensure that adjacent land uses were not incompatible with one another (like a noisy, smoke- and odor-producing factory adjacent to a residential community) and, more generally, to provide that land development in a community produced a harmonious, thought-out pattern over time. In general, land-use controls are the responsibility of cities and suburban municipalities, some of them very small. For small jurisdictions, the use of each tract of land can have a perceptible influence on the community's future, and thus, in exercising its powers to control land use, the municipal government is likely to be concerned entirely with its own future, and not at all with neighboring communities.

Most local governments in the United States are heavily dependent for revenues on the property tax, which is mainly a tax on the value of land and buildings. How much revenue the property tax yields, at a given tax rate, is pretty much determined by how the land within that community is utilized. As suburban development proceeded apace following World War II, it became increasingly clear to local governments that they could use their zoning and similar powers to enhance their fiscal positions and still maintain attractive communities; never mind what this did to adjacent communities.

For example, modern industrial plants and research laboratories are usually physically attractive. They can provide substantial amounts of property tax revenue, and they require very little in the way of local public services. In particular, the plants themselves do not add to school costs, which are heavily supported by the property tax. Thus, communities readily zone for "clean" industry. Also, the ratio of tax revenue to public service costs tends to be high in communities inhabited by high-income families in expensive houses.

At the other extreme, a community composed of moderate-value houses will have a limited tax base, but its families are likely to be relatively young, with large numbers of school-age children. The tax-revenue-to-tax-cost ratio is likely to be highly unfavorable. For example, suppose that a community is spending, net of state and federal aid, $600 for each public school pupil, the funds being raised from the property tax. If the school property tax rate is 2.5 percent of the market value of property, the school taxes on a $25,000 house will be $625. If the typical family has two children in the public schools, there will be a fiscal "loss" of $575 on each such house.

A natural response is to try to set up land-use controls so that only relatively expensive houses can be built in the community. The most popular device has been to zone for large minimum-lot-sizes. At one time, it was assumed that this would guarantee that only expensive houses could be built in the community. Clearly, not every community can be a rich man's enclave. But even if less expensive houses are built on the large lots, this strategy pays fiscal dividends: fewer houses in total can be built in the community, and thus there will be fewer children to educate.

Of course, this raises costs to housing consumers. If minimum-lot-sizes are higher, then the total supply of building lots in an urban area is smaller than it would otherwise be, and the price of a lot is greater. This can be offset by moving further out from the center of the area, but this imposes greater travel costs on consumers, and there is a practical limit to the commuting area, at least until new and faster transportation technology is introduced. Moreover, the local governments on the urban fringe are capable of making the same kinds of calculations that closer-in municipalities have made, and they too quickly require larger minimum-lot-sizes.

The result is an escalation of minimum-lot-sizes in most large metropolitan areas. That this is not a reflection of consumer preferences for spacious living is indicated by the fact that, in most areas, much of the vacant residential land is zoned for lot-sizes far in excess of those on which most people are now living. Builders tend to seek out sites on which they can use the smaller lot-sizes; they build on the larger lots only when unavoidable.

There seem to be only two ways to reverse this trend. One would be to remove land-use powers from small local governments and assign them to county governments, metropolitan-area-wide agencies, or state governments. Another would be to relieve the pressure to maximize the local fiscal situation, by providing more state and federal financing of local public services, especially schools.

Local building codes also serve to increase housing costs unduly, but often this is not so deliberate a policy. Like zoning, building codes were introduced for worthy purposes, to guarantee that minimum construction standards are satisfied. However, they tend to raise costs in a variety of ways. Often, the codes are outmoded and do not permit the use of new materials and techniques. Typically, this is because the requirements are stated in terms of specified materials, rather than performance characteristics—for example, a given thickness of plaster on walls rather than a minimum level of fire resistance. In many cases, building code revision is opposed because of the vested interests of specific building trades and contractors. Another problem is the diversity among local codes, so that large-scale builders operating in several communities cannot standardize techniques and buy materials on a larger scale.

The usual solution suggested is the adoption of uniform statewide codes. There has been limited success in this to date, but it appears likely that there will be great pressure for building code revision in the next few years. A decade from now, this may be a minor problem.

However, we are unlikely to see code restrictions reduced sufficiently to permit really low-standard housing for the poor to be produced in quantity. It should be noted that in many countries, particularly in the underdeveloped parts of the world, poor migrants to urban areas are permitted to build their own housing on vacant land at the edges of the cities. As their incomes rise, they often improve these low-quality houses to the point where they are reasonably decent ones; often governments then provide standard urban utilities, like water, sewers, and electricity. In the United States, our construction standards, designed for middle-class housing, make this impossible.

Yet, there is something to be said for lowering code restrictions. For low-income people, money is much scarcer than time. It is not unreasonable to think that many low-income people would choose to live in the kinds of housing that are most easily improved by their own efforts, as they get money for materials and improvements. This implies two things. First, codes should permit greater use of shell-house construction, in which the builder does little finishing work, but instead leaves it to the buyer. Second, zoning and other provisions should permit, even encourage, the poor to live in the parts of urban areas suitable for single-family or row house shell construction. Instead, we find that most of the new housing constructed for low-income people is in central areas, where the limited availability of land pushes public policy in the direction of high-rise, high-cost, high-subsidy construction. And such housing offers limited opportunities for the occupants to do finishing work themselves.

TAX POLICIES

In many countries, including the United States, governments have at times adopted tax measures designed to encourage housing, by treating some types of housing consumers or investors in housing especially favorably. At the same time, in some countries, *especially* in the United States (and in most other English-speaking countries), governments have employed general tax policies that inadvertently work in the opposite direction, by taxing housing consumption more heavily than other forms of consumption. Property taxes add very substantially to the occupancy costs of housing. Offsetting this, housing expenditure largely escapes state and local government sales taxes, and there are substantial federal income tax advantages offered owner-occupants and certain types of investors in rental housing. On balance, the overall tax system is favorable for owner-occupied housing in suburban areas and unfavorable for other kinds; unfortunately, the favorable situations apply mainly to upper-income people and the unfavorable ones to lower-income people.

To the extent that property taxes on housing are higher than the average tax rate applied to all forms of physical capital, they are similar to other forms of taxes on consumer expenditure—sales and excise taxes—in that they are borne largely by the consumers themselves.[13] By and large, owners of rental housing can and do shift the burden of the tax to renters, through higher rents; homeowners of course bear the burden of the tax themselves. Examined as a sales tax, the housing property tax is a very high one, amounting to high percentages of consumers' current outlays for housing, that is, rents or homeowners' cash outlays for mortgage payments, insurance, heating, and the like. On the average, the tax is equivalent to a sales tax of over 25 percent of consumer expenditure for

---

13. The incidence of the property tax is currently a hotly disputed issue among economists. None, however, deny that differentially high taxes on housing structures are like excise taxes. Because a very considerable portion of all physical capital is *not* subject to property taxation, much of the urban housing stock is in fact subject to differentially high rates of property taxation.

housing, exclusive of the tax itself. The percentages are even higher outside the South and they are especially high in the large urban areas in the Northeast, the Great Lakes states, and California and Oregon; in some places, they are equivalent to a sales tax of as much as 35 percent.

Except for liquor, tobacco, and gasoline, no other use of the consumer dollar is subject to such high rates of tax. Most consumer expenditure is subject to state-local sales taxes of between 3 and 6 percent, and some forms of consumer expenditure, including most services and foreign travel, escape all sales and excise taxation. Thus, consumer taxes raise the price of housing more than they raise the price of other things on which consumers can spend. The evidence strongly indicates that consumers are sensitive to the price of housing—that they consume less housing when its price is higher. This is not to imply that a family will live in smaller quarters; instead, it will occupy lower-quality housing or housing in a less attractive and hence cheaper part of the urban area.

But consider the offsets. First, most housing expenditure is not subject to the ordinary sales taxes. Second, and far more important, are the federal income tax advantages of home ownership. Mortgage interest and property taxes are deductible in computing federal income taxes. Also, there is what economists call the "imputed income" from owner-occupied housing, which escapes income tax. Any homeowner has some equity investment in his house. He could sell his house and become a renter, investing his equity in securities or savings deposits. However, the income from this investment is taxable, unlike the equivalent imputed income in the form of housing services from investment in an owner-occupied house.

Table 4-4 illustrates, with hypothetical examples, the tax consequences of differing decisions with regard to housing, for a family of four with an annual income of $10,000. A

typical homeowner family like this might live in a $22,000
house, having an outstanding mortgage of $12,000, an equity
of $10,000 and annual housing outlays of nearly $2,300. It

TABLE 4-4   *Tax Treatment of Family of Four with $10,000 Income
Making Differing Housing Decisions*

	Living in $22,000 Housing Unit		Living in $15,000 Housing Unit[a]	
	Owned	Rented	Owned	Rented
Annual Housing Costs or Rent	$ 2,260	$2,260	$1,540	$1,540
Expenditure on Items Subject to Sales Tax	3,000	3,000	3,720	3,720
Equity in House at Beginning of Year	10,000	—	6,800	—
Additional Income from Investment at 5 Percent, Instead of House Equity	—	500	—	340
Taxes:				
Local Property Tax (3 Percent of Value)	660	660[b]	450	450[b]
State-Local Sales Taxes (5 Percent)	150	150	186	186
Federal Income Tax[c]	757	986	849	960
TOTAL	$ 1,567	$1,796	$1,485	$1,596

Source: Based on relations among income, house value, mortgage characteristics, and monthly housing costs for mortgaged homeowner properties in *U.S.
Census of Housing: 1960.*

[a]All items in last two columns, except federal income tax and sales taxes, are
68 percent of the comparable items in the first two columns; the $15,000 house
value is 68 percent of $22,000.

[b]Paid as part of monthly rent and not deductible on federal income tax returns.

[c]Based on 1972 federal tax rates. Renter families are assumed to take the
standard deduction. Homeowner families are assumed to have $750 in itemized
deductions aside from the mortgage interest, sales tax, and local property tax
deductions.

might spend $3,000 a year on items subject to the ordinary
sales tax; at 5 percent, this would cost the family $150 a year.

Now suppose the family, instead of owning, rented a house
or apartment with the same value and housing costs. If it in-

vested the $10,000 equity in a form yielding 5 percent, its taxable income would be $500 higher; in addition, it would not be able to deduct mortgage interest or property payments, although it would be shouldering the latter indirectly, through rental payments. Its federal income tax payments would be $229 higher than a comparable homeowner family. In other words, for the homeowner family, federal income tax savings offset about one-third of the property tax payments; for the renter family, there is no such offset.

Another way of looking at this is to consider a similar family choosing to live in cheaper housing (illustrated in the last two columns of Table 4-4), and choosing to spend instead more money on goods subject to the sales tax, like clothing or a more expensive car. The property tax burden would decline, but income and sales tax payments would be higher. For the homeowner, $128 of the $210 reduction in property taxes would be offset by higher income and sales taxes. For the renter family, hardly any of the reduction in the property tax burden paid through rent would be offset by increased sales and income taxes. Thus, on balance, homeowners have little tax incentive to reduce housing expenditure, but renters do have a real tax incentive to keep their housing consumption low.

The income tax is the critical feature. Since income taxes rise as a percentage of income as income rises, the net tax treatment tends to be very favorable to high-income families and very unfavorable to low-income families. Moreover, low-income families tend to be renters rather than homeowners, and the net tax treatment of all tenants is unfavorable.

There is also a geographic dimension. In large central cities, a substantial portion of the housing stock is rental housing, while in suburban areas (and in smaller central cities), home-ownership is overwhelmingly dominant. Moreover, in suburbs, property tax payments are visibly linked to the public services families enjoy—schools, streets, police protection, parks, and so on. Thus, the family can treat the property tax as a payment for a district "package" of services. In large central cities, in contrast, the population, property types, and public services provided are so diverse that it is difficult for any given family, especially renters, to sensibly link its own property tax burden to the specific public services it uses.

The overall result, therefore, is that the tax system tends to discourage housing consumption in large central cities, except for high-income homeowners who make up a very small portion of central-city housing consumers. Were central-city property taxes on housing substantially lower, rents would be lower and housing consumption would be expanded, chiefly in the form of higher-quality housing for middle-income families in response to greater demand. This has positive effects on lower-income city dwellers, by freeing for them the housing formerly occupied by middle-income families. Indeed, it has been argued that the single most effective strategy for improving the housing conditions of the central-city poor is to expand rapidly the total supply of housing, even if little of the *new* housing is for the poor. Among American urban areas, the greatest housing improvements for the poor have occurred, not where the increase in the stock of low-rent public housing has been greatest, but where the total supply has increased most.

In belated recognition of the effects of taxation on housing, governments have offered some forms of tax reduction on housing. Property taxes are not paid on low-rent public housing (in contrast, tenants in public housing in Britain do pay property taxes). There is usually provision for tax abatement in state government middle-income housing programs; the New York State program now authorizes complete property tax exemption, for example. But such programs inevitably in-volve restrictions designed to ensure that the tax advantages accrue only to projects and occupants meeting various condi-tions, like income limits. There is reason to believe that more general tax reduction on central-city housing would be a highly effective policy.

This is in keeping with economists' usual preferences for changing the rules of the game in general, rather than trying to manipulate tax and other instruments in a highly tailored way. The latter policy is costly and awkward to administer and will rule out participants who marginally fail to satisfy the detailed conditions of a program or who cannot afford the lengthy delays that are customary. In contrast, changes of general application, like reductions in the property tax deter-rent to rental housing consumption, open the action to all sorts of private investors and consumers who can exercise their initiative, and their differing preferences, in a more favorable environment. The issue is an old one: in a highly complex society and economy, decentralized (including private) deci-sion making on details is essential; very detailed, centralized decision making simply does not work well in socialist as well as capitalist societies.

One set of general tax reduction rules with effects on hous-ing is found in the federal income tax treatment of those who invest in rental housing. These provisions apply to investment in general and were designed for industrial, rather than real estate, investment. The principal feature is the one that allows investors to take deductions from taxable income for property depreciation at rates that are faster than the rates at which buildings actually depreciate in physical terms; this accelerated depreciation cycle can start all over again every time a build-ing is sold to a new owner. This is especially attractive for real estate investors, because they rely heavily on borrowed money;

a small investment of their own funds can produce heavy cash returns after tax.

The trouble with this is twofold. First, the economics of this, depending as they do on substantial cash rental flows, are much more favorable to investment in luxury apartments or office buildings than in low- and moderate-income housing; there has been much urban construction to secure these tax advantages, but almost none of it has been in the less expensive sector of the housing market. Second, there is a real incentive for quick turnover of rental property to skim off the tax advantages, and an inducement to minimize maintenance and other costs.

Reforms in these and other federal income tax provisions, to minimize unnecessary tax advantages for low-priority real estate investment and to encourage better repair and rehabilitation of rental housing, have been proposed.[14] Also, there are proposals for much larger, more tailored tax incentives for private investment in low-income housing and for income tax penalties on poorly maintained buildings. Some observers, however, argue that any such tax incentives and penalties are likely to be blunt, inefficient policy instruments with unexpected side effects, and that the real urban housing problems must be attacked head on, rather than in this indirect way:

> The essential economic cost and resource allocation problems involved in paying for subsidizing low-income urban housing is [sic] not magically waved away or transmuted by translating the costs into tax concessions, particularly if they are not well-suited to accomplish the precise job demanded to rebuild the inner cities.[15]

---

14. See Richard E. Slitor, *The Federal Income Tax in Relation to Housing*, National Commission on Urban Problems, Research Report no. 5, 1968, pp. 103–108.
15. Slitor, *The Federal Income Tax*, p. 112.

THE PRIVATE LANDLORD AS VILLAIN

A fifth group of housing policies deals with the problems associated with the existing stock of privately owned rental housing on the presumption that socially unacceptable economic behavior by private landlords is a, if not *the,* major difficulty. The notion that greedy landlords charge unconscionably high rents for shoddy and ill-maintained inner-city housing occupied by less well-off families is not a new one in this country. Awareness of the dismal housing provided by private landlords for foreign immigrants to the larger cities around the beginning of the twentieth century was the initial stimulus to the very first movement for public intervention into urban housing markets, the movement that led to the adoption of municipal laws, or housing codes, setting minimum standards of housing safety and decency. The landlord again seemed the villain of the piece with the large-scale migration of minority-group poor households to big central cities in the 1950s and 1960s, a group who provided a market for very low-quality housing at seemingly high rents. And, in any city, the landlord can appear villainous indeed if a period of low housing construction coincides with rising incomes (and thus rising housing demand). This permits very rapid increases in rents, as for example occurred during World War II, or would have occurred in the absence of the rent controls then imposed.

By the end of the Korean War, rent controls had ended in the United States, except in New York State where they persist to this day (in New York City, nearly 1.7 million of the 2 million privately owned renter-occupied housing units are still subject to some form of rent control). In Western Europe, however, rent controls originally imposed during World War II, or even World War I, are still in effect; they are common also in many large cities in developing countries. In the late 1960s, sharp increases in rents led to a clamor for the re-imposition of rent controls, and controls were in fact imposed in a number of cities, such as Boston and Hartford. Interestingly, some of the most vigorous campaigns for rent control have been in smaller cities that house large universities, like Cambridge and Berkeley. This no doubt results from three factors: the fact that students are, in the nature of things, renters and increasingly live in off-campus apartments; the increased student interest in local politics (facilitated by the lowering of the voting age); and perhaps the ease with which landlords can be made the targets of radical rhetoric.

Economists generally agree that rent control is bad long-run housing policy, for it discourages construction of new rental housing if the rents on new housing are controlled, or threatened with control sooner or later. Perhaps as important, rent control discourages adequate maintenance of existing housing, because controlled apartments can be rented with less-than-adequate maintenance if the legal maximum rent is below the market rent even for poorly maintained apartments. Elaborate efforts to administer rent controls so as to compel adequate maintenance in New York and some European cities have had very limited success. As a short-run measure, the economic effects of rent control are quite different, especially if the impetus to rent control is the inability to build new housing, as in wartime.[16] The economic costs of short-run

---

16. One argument advanced for rent control in London and some other places is that no significant investment in rental housing will occur, even without rent control, because of tax laws, alternative investment opportunities, and declining inner-city populations. If this is the case (and American central-city experience is *not* consistent with this assumption), then rent control will do less harm than it would were the investment outlook more optimistic.

rent control are not serious, because deferring upkeep for brief periods generally does no lasting damage to the housing stock. The economic benefits relate to income distribution: if demand is strong and the housing supply cannot be increased, as in wartime, the resulting rapid increases in rents will transfer income from tenants to owners without beneficial resource allocation effects.

In general, rent control amounts to a form of tax on the owners of existing housing, with the proceeds given to tenants. Some justify this form of taxation on the grounds that landlords are richer than tenants. It is not clear that this is always, or even largely, true. In 1970, half the renter-occupied housing units in central cities were in buildings with four or fewer apartments, and 63 percent in buildings with fewer than ten apartments. Many such buildings are owned by older landlords of modest means whose main source of income is the rental property itself. Another, perhaps more defensible, argument for rent control lies in the limited options open to the central city: it cannot afford vast housing programs for low-income families, nor can it compel the suburbs to open their gates to the central-city poor. It can control rents here and now, never mind the adverse long-run effects.

There have been few empirical studies of the actual economic consequences of rent control. One, done for New York City as of 1968, estimates that rent control resulted in occupants consuming 4.4 percent less housing services and close to 10 percent more in other goods and services than they would have consumed without rent control. Rent control in effect increased their real incomes by an average of 3.4 percent, with poorer families receiving significantly larger benefits than richer families. However, the estimated cost to landlords, in lost income or capital values, was double the benefits to tenants. Thus, the income-transfer process was economically inefficient, and the estimate of economic waste was $250 million annually.[17]

Rent controls aggravate the problem of undermaintaining existing housing, but that problem exists much more widely in inner cities, even where there is no rent control. Reducing upkeep expenses may be the only way for landlords to operate profitably when the only demand for the housing they own is from low-income families able to pay modest rents. Indeed, the classic way in which lower-income families have been housed in cities has been by the "trickling down" of good housing once occupied by the rich or the middle class, housing that is in neighborhoods that are no longer attractive or of types that are no longer considered desirable by families that can afford alternatives. Usually, the trickling down is accompanied by reduced upkeep efforts.

In the 1950s and 1960s, many cities attempted to combat this housing "disinvestment" by stepped-up enforcement of housing codes. These efforts have been less than successful in two ways. First, the enforcement effort itself is exceptionally difficult and requires expensive inspections and lengthy litigation in a crowded court system. Second, where the incomes of the tenants are inadequate to support the rental levels required by "like-new" maintenance efforts, rigid enforcement can lead to abandonment of buildings by owners. If an owner is compelled to lose money on a building and if the prospect is for

---

17. Edgar O. Olsen, "An Econometric Analysis of Rent Control," *Journal of Political Economy* 80 (November–December 1972). The loss to landlords is greater than the benefits to tenants because both the rent per unit of housing and the quantity of housing services consumed is reduced; revenue to landlords equals price (P) times quantity (Q). Tenants do not gain the entire sum, PQ, because presumably they would have preferred to consume more housing in a free market, and less of other goods and services; there is some loss to tenants in the form of distortion of their preferred consumption patterns, offsetting the gain in reduced rents.

never-ending losses, then the building has no capital value: the owner quite rationally will ignore the sunk costs and decline to throw good money after bad.

As indicated in Chapter 2, rigid enforcement of codes is by no means the sole cause of the large-scale abandonment phenomenon observed in many inner-city neighborhoods. High, and rising, property taxes, interest rates, fire insurance rates and repair costs, difficulties in refinancing mortgages, and vandalism when apartments become vacant all contribute. But rigid code enforcement surely cannot solve any significant part of the housing problem, as long as tenants are unable to pay the economic costs that literal adherence to housing codes entails.

Like so many other economic problems, this too is not an either-or situation. More modest housing code requirements, with commensurately lower upkeep expenses, might be consistent with the income levels of inner-city families. An intensive study of rental housing in inner-city Baltimore found that many landlords were effective managers who found it possible to combine modest upkeep efforts with marginally *lower* rents than were found in the more poorly maintained houses in the same areas. The secret was that the good managers had virtually no vacancies and experienced little vandalism. The conclusion was that the city should support good management by reasonable code enforcement efforts, more realistic property tax levels, and some assistance with financing. The most important finding was the crucial role of management. This led to recommendations that the city assist in shifting ownership of rental housing in the inner city to better hands: to the professional, private owner-managers who had proven themselves and to cooperatives formed among tenants.[18]

---

18. Michael A. Stegman, *Housing Investment in the Inner City: The Dynamics of Decline* (Cambridge, Mass.: The M.I.T. Press, 1972).

Conversion of rental housing to cooperative or condominium ownership has been a strong trend in the middle- and
upper-income housing stock in recent years, in good part
because the federal income tax advantages of ownership are so
substantial in those income ranges. Increasingly, there is interest in cooperative conversion of lower-income rental housing,
along the lines of the Stegman proposal. In this case, the income tax advantages are not important. What is important is
getting the properties out of the hands of demoralized and/or
incompetent owner-managers (who are often elderly white
owners of buildings occupied by black and Spanish tenants).
The hope is that the cooperators will become more concerned
with, and sympathetic to, management problems once they
share in ownership and even that, where the buildings are
small ones (as is the case in Baltimore), the cooperators will
be able to do more of the small-scale maintenance work themselves. It is by no means clear that these hopes can be realized
on a large scale. There have been isolated successes in some
American cities, and fairly good experience in some Latin
American cities, but managing multifamily buildings is by no
means easy, even for the rich and well-informed who occupy
most of the nearly 250,000 cooperative or condominium
apartments that now exist in American central cities.

Housing Allowances

Most of the housing policies we have examined do not have
much effect on the housing problems of the urban poor;
indeed, most are not designed to do so. And those that are
suffer from major defects: either they are costly and limited in
scope (like public housing) or they run aground on the hard
fact of low income itself. But, as we have seen, there are
grounds for skepticism about the effectiveness of a simple

income-transfer strategy in solving the housing problems of the poor in American cities. Not surprisingly, there is now considerable interest in a hybrid strategy, one in which low-income families are provided with additional money that must be used for housing purposes under conditions designed to prevent simply bidding up rents for existing undermaintained apartments. The general term for this strategy is "housing allowances."

One type of housing allowance, enacted in 1965, is the federal rent supplement program. Under the program, eligible families pay 25 percent of their incomes for rent, while the federal government pays directly to landlords the difference between the economic rent levels and the tenants' payments. It has several advantages. It ties the subsidy to the family, not to the housing unit, and thus keys the amount of subsidy to the specific needs of each family. It also shifts the responsibility for building and operating low-rent housing from the local authorities to private groups. It makes it possible, in theory at least, to avoid economic segregation, because there is no need for all the families in a building or project to be poor; those who are not poor pay the market rents. Moreover, poor families need not move out if their incomes rise, as is the case with public housing. Their rental payments rise and eventually the subsidy disappears.

The program provides for very "deep" subsidies to individual families, conceivably twice as great as to those in public housing, and reaches families with incomes as low as $2,000. Although once espoused by conservatives, because it presumably is less "socialistic" than public housing, it has not been popular in Congress. Partly, this may be because of the extent of subsidy; partly it is because of opposition to the degree of racial integration implicit in a program that permits people with very different incomes to live in the same building. At

any rate, the program has been encumbered with many restrictions, and the funds authorized for it have been small. The
number of new housing units actually started and completed
under the program during its first eight years was only about
120,000.[19]

The rent supplement program, like most other federal housing programs, was meant to be a housing *production* program.
Housing allowances, however, need not be tied to the production of new housing. Indeed, the early proponents of rent
supplements here and abroad advocated programs that would
permit poor families to live in existing housing of a type and
quality now beyond their economic reach. A more generalized
program of housing allowances might aim at three components of the existing housing stock.

First, most central cities have a fair amount of existing
underutilized housing for which the market demand is limited.
Typically this housing is in older neighborhoods beyond the
true slums and is inhabited by an aging, lower-middle-class
white population. In some cities there is a good supply of
large apartments in such neighborhoods; in others, there are
old, moderately large one- and two-family houses. Histori-
cally, economic pressures have resulted in the subdivision of
these into small units, and they have been rented by lower-
income families, white or otherwise. Many low-income families are large and thus overcrowd the small apartments.
Overcrowding of small units in buildings that were not well-
suited for subdividing to begin with greatly speeds their
deterioration, and the deterioration of large numbers of buildings in a neighborhood can quickly convert it into a new slum.

---

19. In contrast, the subsidized-interest-rate programs under the Housing Act
of 1968 (Sections 235 and 236) produced nearly ten times as many housing starts in their first four years.

Housing allowances could enable large low-income families to move into *unsubdivided* houses and apartments in such neighborhoods; if this were done in limited numbers in any given neighborhood, the conversion of it into a true slum area could be avoided, and, perhaps, some racial integration could be achieved as well.

Second, this mechanism might also be used to enable low-income central-city families to move into older suburban areas, or even to occupy some apartments in new garden-type developments in suburban areas, apartments aimed at middle-income tenants. The racial integration involved in this no doubt would be hotly opposed by all-white suburban communities. Nonetheless, it is one of the few policy instruments conceivably available to promote any degree of racial, combined with economic, integration. That goal may be quixotic, but it continues to be professed by many in our society.

Third, and most important, housing allowances would provide the financial resources to support adequate maintenance of the deteriorating—but not hopeless—housing that very large numbers of central-city poor families now live in. It is doubtful whether the priority housing need of those large central cities with declining populations is a large volume of newly constructed housing within city boundaries. Rather, it is preservation of the very large stocks of housing built to middle-class standards during the 1910–1930 period, housing now threatened by the combination of low tenant incomes, rising operating costs, and owner demoralization, leading to undermaintenance, vacancies, vandalism, and, ultimately, to abandonment. Perhaps the most thoroughgoing analysis of the problem was that made by the New York City Rand Institute, in connection with the major revision of New York City's rent-control law in 1971. The analysis had several steps. First, the economic costs of the existing rent-controlled housing stock, assuming adequate levels of maintenance, were estimated. Second, the rents necessary to support such economic costs were estimated and set as the target "maximum base rents" for the revised rent-control law. Third, the rents were compared to the incomes of the tenants. Fourth, an estimate was made of the aggregate difference between the required rents and the rents that would be paid if no tenants had to face excessive rent-to-income ratios. This estimate—$195 million, to roughly 500,000 families—is an indication of the appropriate scope and magnitude of a housing allowance plan for New York City, as of 1968.[20]

Estimates of the costs and coverage of a similar national housing allowance plan based on 1967 price and income levels have been made by Henry J. Aaron.[21] This plan provides for a housing allowance that is equal to the difference between shelter costs in each region (as measured by the Bureau of Labor Statistics low standard of living budget) and one-fourth of income. Aaron estimates that such a plan would have covered 12.3 million households and cost $4.9 billion in 1967, if housing prices were not bid up at all by the housing allowance plan (if housing costs rose by 10 percent, the program cost would have risen by 25 percent and the households covered by 15 percent). Much of the benefit would have accrued to people living in rural areas and small towns. However, 4.7 million central-city households, nearly one-fourth of all such households, would have received allowances totaling $1.9 billion.

In both the Rand plan for New York and the Aaron plan,

---

20. Ira S. Lowry, ed., *Rental Housing in New York City,* vol. I, *Confronting the Crisis* (New York City Rand Institute, February 1970).

21. Henry J. Aaron, *Shelter and Subsidies: Who Benefits from Federal Housing Policies?* (Washington, D.C.: The Brookings Institution, 1972), pp. 167–173.

annual allowances per household would average roughly $400, which is far below the average assistance per household in the existing federal housing programs aimed at low-income families. This low cost per family is one advantage, as are the ability to reach *all* low-income families, not just a lucky few, and the avoidance of tying the allowance to a specific housing unit, thus precluding individual families from making decisions that would improve their own housing status further. A good deal of effort is now being given to the precise design of housing allowance schemes, and the federal government is now supporting a variety of experimental housing allowance plans, in large-scale social experimentation parallel to experiments with the negative income tax (see Chapter 3). To many economists, housing allowances seem one of those rare policy options that combine equity and efficiency.[22]

Conclusion

There are two principal lessons to be learned from this review of housing policies. First, the simplistic assumption that a single policy instrument can solve *the* urban housing problem is clearly false. A number of policies, new and traditional, some of them having a modest impact on the underlying problems, seems necessary if there is to be be a massive overall impact.

---

22. It may be asked why there should be both a negative income tax and a housing allowance plan of similar design that extends beyond the income range of the former and encourages recipients to spend more on housing than they would have chosen if left to their own devices. The answer lies in the very existence of so many public programs that concentrate on housing conditions. As one observer puts it, "the declared interest in housing standards (in contrast with the silence about adequate provision of many other goods) implies society's greater concern with adequate housing." Henry J. Aaron, *Why Is Welfare So Hard to Reform?* (Washington, D.C.: The Brookings Institution, 1973), p. 63.

Second, there is need to avoid contradictory policies, considering here both the policies explicitly aimed at housing conditions and those affecting housing more or less accidentally. Examples include the adverse effects of urban renewal heretofore on the supply of low-rent housing, the impact of the property tax on central-city rental housing, and the effects of zoning restrictions and high-standard building codes. Moreover, it does not seem at all efficient to adopt new policy instruments in order to counteract the adverse effects of old ones. Repealing laws on occasion may be more effective than passing new ones. Here, as in most aspects of urban economic policy, the need is for careful analysis of costs and benefits and rejection of the idea that old institutions must be accepted as is, because they are there.

At the outset of this chapter, attention was drawn to three key housing problems: housing for the poor in cities, the aging neighborhoods, and the limited range of housing choice in many urban areas for most families. The first problem has been treated head-on, by discussing income, housing cost, and housing supply strategies. The second and third problems have been treated only inferentially.

If housing cost and supply policies lead to dramatic expansion in effective housing demand, then it is a fair presumption that the aging gray areas surrounding the slums could be transformed by the pressure of market demand into attractive residential locations once again. This has happened to close-in, highly accessible neighborhoods in several cities, but largely for high-income residents. The policies discussed earlier could do this for more ordinary sections. And, in the process, families will find that decent housing at moderate cost with adequate neighborhood amenities can be found without enormous sacrifice of accessibility.

These two heretofore neglected problems, however, are not

simply housing problems. They concern the ways in which urban land is used, about which there has been much conflict and all too little economic analysis. The use of urban land and the policies affecting it (including urban renewal) is the major theme of the next chapter.

5

The Use of Urban Land

Good buildings are a necessary, but insufficient, condition for good neighborhoods, good cities, and good suburbs. Public policies to shape the use of urban land are necessary, and we have had such policies for most of this century, in the form of zoning, subdivision controls, master plans, and, more recently, urban renewal. Public decision making on housing policies has involved a fair amount of economic calculation, although the calculations have often been wrong. Public decision making on urban land use rarely has been based on such explicit economic reasoning. The land-use decisions made by private parties in the marketplace on the basis of their own individual economic calculations are perceived to generate external or social disadvantages in many instances, to be overcome by physical controls, legal proscriptions, and public spending in the pursuit of loosely defined planners' ideals or community goods. Economics has seemed the province of asocial or antisocial individual actions, not a method of analysis to be applied to the public actions required to promote efficiency and equity in urban land use.

Increasingly—in large part in reaction to the early decisions made in the urban renewal program—economic analysis is

150

being applied to land-use policy decisions. This chapter is devoted to discussion of the economic implications of such decisions and the use of economic tools to improve public policy. No pat answers are offered, for the economic theory of the spatial organization of urban areas is far from fully developed and the models needed to apply even the simplest of theory to the enormously complex phenomena that constitute a real-life metropolis are still in their infancy.

Renewing City Neighborhoods

At a given moment in time, a city has two basic sets of resources. There are its people, their talents, and their institutions, whether business, public, or social. Its other asset is its land surface, which amounts to a collection of locations, each with unique characteristics. To a considerable extent, a city's future depends upon its ability to induce people and organizations to use those locations to best advantage, from various standpoints: the functioning of the city's economy; satisfaction of the social, cultural, and aesthetic needs of the city's population; minimizing fiscal costs and maximizing fiscal returns. These objectives are often in conflict with one another.

Urban renewal is best considered as a strategy designed to resolve these conflicts and achieve these objectives by changing present land uses to more suitable ones. The instruments available are the powers governments have to condemn land, the federally subsidized write-down of land values, and other subsidy and control devices. Ideally, the strategy will maximize opportunities for benefits external to the specific sites on which public funds and energies are expended. That is, private reuse of adjacent sites will be encouraged, so that whole neighborhoods are changed.

Land uses in cities change all the time, without public intervention or subsidy. Sometimes the changes are unattractive ones, for example, when middle- and upper-class residential neighborhoods decay into slums. But often the privately induced changes are for the better, involving more intensive use of sites or uses for which they are more suitable. This happens continually in and around central business districts. A natural question is: why not permit the market to function? If neighborhoods are deteriorating, why not let them decay to the point at which the land is very cheap, and private redevelopers will step in to exploit the advantages the market then affords?

One argument for public intervention is a very pragmatic one. Land ownership in cities is very fragmented, and therefore it is often difficult to assemble land on a private basis. In a deteriorating section, as noted in Chapter 4, redevelopment of small scattered sites is not very likely to make much sense, because the surrounding deterioration will limit the market attractiveness of the redeveloped site. Private developers therefore will act only if they can acquire fairly large tracts of land, such as whole city blocks. But a single owner will often hold out. In some cases, private redevelopers will pay an exorbitant price to the holdout; in others, they may be able to build around the holdout. However, in many instances, the holdout can frustrate the whole enterprise. Use of public power to condemn land, that is, to purchase it despite the unwillingness of the owner to sell, can overcome this obstacle.

It has been pointed out[1] that it is seldom necessary to acquire *all* the property in a blighted area in order to internalize a large part of the benefits from redevelopment and that individual properties can be, and often are, acquired by private redevelopers through mechanisms that conceal the fact that

---

1. By Edwin S. Mills in *Urban Economics* (Chicago: Scott, Foresman, 1972), p. 174.

large-scale redevelopment is in prospect. Use of the public condemnation power thus may not be absolutely essential to success, but it does raise the probability of success. The higher this probability, the sooner private redevelopers will act.

A more general argument for public intervention relates to the external damages caused by blighted areas. Areas surrounding the most seriously blighted ones become less attractive over time, and individual property owners can do little to offset this. Public intervention to redevelop the seriously blighted sections can protect the surrounding areas, preserving and even enhancing their natural advantages.

A vital consideration here is the dimension of time. While the worst areas are deteriorating to the point that they are cheap enough to redevelop without public intervention, the external damages are mounting. The process may go on for many years. But given that most of us have a positive "time preference"—a preference for benefits enjoyed now over benefits realized years hence (see Chapter 1)—there can be a strong case for *not* waiting until the "natural" market process works itself out, even if public subsidy is required to achieve immediate reuse of blighted land.

Suppose that the rate of interest, expressing the preference for benefits realized now rather than at a future date, is 6 percent a year. Suppose also that the total external benefits to residents, businesses, and property owners in a city from redeveloping a severely run-down section were $1 million annually, in the form of higher property values, more attractive surroundings, higher tax payments, and the like. Suppose, too, that the city had to wait twenty years for private redevelopment. The $1 million in annual benefits twenty years hence has a present value of only $312,000 discounted at 6 percent interest annually. The city as a community should be willing to subsidize redevelopment by up to $688,000 a year in order to obtain those benefits now rather than twenty years from now. Tax payments totaling $688,000 a year could pay off a bond issue of more than $9 million over twenty years. Thus, if the city were to borrow $9 million and use it to subsidize immediate redevelopment, the community would be better off than if it waited twenty years for unsubsidized redevelopment.

This kind of reasoning does not automatically justify every proposed urban renewal effort. In each case, it is necessary to compare the external benefits realized by the community at large with the subsidy costs and with the costs imposed on those displaced by the reuse of the land; in most cases, such costs are compensated (from the subsidy funds) only to a very limited extent. For example, most low-income people displaced from urban renewal sites end up spending, involuntarily, a great deal more for housing than they did before. The housing is likely to be higher in quality, but the decision to spend more was not one that was willingly made by those displaced.

Truly comprehensive calculations of benefits and costs might indicate that a fair number of the projects undertaken under the federal urban renewal program were ill-advised. It was pointed out in Chapter 4 that the federal program has not really been a rehousing program (although much of the land is used for housing purposes eventually). In fact, it has burdened displaced residents, and small businesses serving them, with substantial uncompensated costs. Conceivably, the renewal might have taken place even in the absence of subsidy. If so, the net benefits strictly attributable to the subsidy are very small.

Such projects are undertaken largely because the subsidy is mainly a federal one, rather than a local one; no doubt in most such cases the benefits exceeded the subsidy costs to local governments. For example, the local community benefits from subsidized downtown renewal, even when that makes no economic sense for the nation as a whole. Federally subsidized downtown commercial redevelopment usually involves more elegant design standards than is the case with ordinary privately financed development, a benefit to the community paid for largely by the federal subsidy. Can federal subsidy be justified, then? It is clear that there is a national interest in the welfare of low-income people, no matter where they live; in pursuance of this interest, the federal government subsidizes hundreds of thousands of low-income families under various housing programs by amounts that now average close to $1,000 a year. But, as we have seen, the federal urban renewal program hurts rather than helps low-income people, on balance.

It is hard to see the *nation*wide interest in subsidizing specific changes in land use in a given city. There is some metropolitan *region*wide interest in better land use in a given central city, because the whole metropolitan economy may be made to function better if the central city's land is more efficiently utilized. However, we have very few local governments operating over entire metropolitan regions, and state governments are generally inactive in the field of urban land use. Thus, the central cities are on their own. Being hard pressed for fiscal resources, they appeal to the federal government. The federal program then is a substitute for regional programs that might make more sense. The federal program is an inferior substitute, however, in that it has surely encouraged projects that would *not* have been undertaken had the metropolitan area itself been compelled to do the subsidizing on its own.

Another criticism of urban renewal as it has operated in the United States is that it has tended toward uniformity of treatment of different projects. In a broad-gauge urban renewal program, there are at least three constraints a government faces. First, there is usually a limit on the total amount of public subsidy available for all projects combined over a period of years. Second, there is a very stringent limitation on the amount of governmental entrepreneurial energy that can be applied, for the supply of talented, innovative, effective administrators is very limited. Third, each site is unique; if it is utilized for one purpose, it is not available for others.

This implies that there should be differing degrees of public intervention at each renewal site. On some sites, there might be little subsidy, although a higher subsidy project might have a higher payoff on each of those sites. However, a small subsidy would free funds and energies for other sites where only a very high subsidy project can work at all. Other sites might be left without subsidy, for private development. Thus, governments might assist with land assembly in highly accessible areas with potential for private redevelopment, but offer no subsidy. In less choice neighborhoods that are still in relatively good shape, modest subsidies might be offered, while in the least desirable neighborhoods, massive subsidy might be applied—for example, writing down the land value to zero and providing subsidies for construction costs.

It should be noted that the purpose of subsidizing urban renewal is not to subsidize the individuals or businesses who will occupy the redeveloped site. Instead, the subsidy can be viewed as having one of three possible purposes, depending on the nature of the project. First, subsidized urban renewal in central business districts can be considered a means to accelerate the necessary adjustment of downtowns to the new land uses consistent with the decentralization of population and economic activity in urban areas. As we have seen, speeding the adjustment process can be highly worthwhile, but it is not necessarily so. To be truly successful, a downtown renewal project must lead to improvement (usually indicated by increased land values) in blocks and sections adjacent to the project. As Edwin S. Mills has put it:

> The essence of the justification for public intervention to speed adjustment to new equilibrium uses of downtown land is that, if the public sector increases the productivity of land in renewal areas, it will increase the productivity of neighboring sites by increasing the jobs and other activities to which they are accessible.[2]

Second, urban renewal can be viewed as a wealth transfer, not to the new owners or occupants, but to the previous owners whose property has declined in value as the area has deteriorated (or as retail shopping decentralized away from downtown areas). It is frequently observed that property prices in areas where urban renewal is expected are well above what would appear to be the economic value of the property in present or unsubsidized alternative uses. Of course, this purpose of urban renewal is never openly stated, for few people would agree that this type of subsidy is a valid use of funds raised by general taxation.

Third, the subsidy in urban renewal can be considered in effect a bribe to induce people to occupy sites in urban locations that they would have shunned in the absence of the bribe. In particular, the subsidy may be a bribe to induce middle-income families to live in central-city neighborhoods, rather than in distant suburbs. To repeat, the rationale for the bribe is that there are benefits to the community at large from such a land-use pattern, specifically, from making the graying areas of the inner city attractive places in which to live, rather than discarded neighborhoods housing only those too poor to have any other alternative. If the poor are not to be hurt fur-

---

2. Mills, *Urban Economics,* p. 189.

ther, there must be alternatives for them. One such alternative, discussed below, is to provide much more housing for low- and modest-income families beyond the central city.

Urban renewal subsidies are not likely to be sufficient, by themselves, to make the gray areas of central cities attractive for middle-income families with children. The subsidies can make housing cheaper than it would otherwise be, but a policy confined to cheap housing may be of limited effectiveness. This is suggested by the fact that middle-income suburban residents spend much higher fractions of their incomes for housing than do middle-income central-city residents, by and large. The higher expenditure for housing in the suburbs, however, buys all sorts of amenities not available in the city: more openness; usually, a feeling of newness; often, better schools and other public services; better access to recreational opportunities, especially for children; and much greater ease of automobile ownership and use, which is an essential ingredient of middle-class American living.

Central-city neighborhoods seldom can reproduce the suburban amenities precisely. What they can do, instead, is offer substitutes for some of the amenities, offsetting advantages (such as greater accessibility to downtown opportunities), and amelioration of the worst disadvantages. For example, they can provide more publicly owned recreational facilities to substitute for the large lots and open space in the outer areas. They can be redeveloped with medium-density, rather than high-density, housing, types that are more suitable for families with children and less hostile to automobile ownership, albeit at higher cost. Schools and municipal housekeeping can be improved to match suburban standards.

All this is likely to take a great deal of public money, money that central cities find it hard indeed to raise under present conditions. Ultimately, this will be possible only if the system of financing urban public services is overhauled, as will be suggested in Chapter 8. More immediately, if the gray areas are in fact redeveloped, central-city tax bases will be expanded; there is every reason to believe that middle-income neighborhoods in central cities can be as much self-financed as are middle-income suburbs.

In addition, there is the issue of the choice of strategies. Some of the funds for improvements in amenities and public services can be diverted from the housing subsidies necessary if the central city were to rely instead on a strategy confined to cheap housing as a bribe. New York City (until recently) was a classic example of the cheap-housing strategy, with rent control on old middle-income housing and heavy subsidies for new middle-income housing. Both housing policies tended to depress the city's revenues, thus making it difficult indeed to finance adequate public services. The cheap-housing strategy in New York was not notably successful, except in making it possible for childless households (most of whom are wedded to the central city anyhow) to live less expensively.

The very large central cities have a potential for redevelopment that only recently has become available. The enormous growth in office activities in the American economy is what explains private redevelopment of central business districts in recent years. Increasing employment in office activities has led to the construction of new office buildings; the high incomes of the downtown office workers have spilled over into the retail and services establishments downtown, so that downtown shopping in the largest cities has kept up well, despite the increasing decentralization of the population away from the central cities. White-collar employment has also increased in the suburbs. Large numbers of new office buildings, large and small, have been built in suburban areas, often in conjunction with regional shopping centers.

Close to 90 percent of the growth in employment in the American economy since 1950 has been in white-collar occupations. In 1965, there were 28 million Americans employed in office-type occupations; by the year 2000, there should be 59 million so employed.[3] Many of these jobs will be in central corporate offices, large financial institutions, and other management and control organizations located in downtown sections of the very large cities. Many more will be scattered about the suburban parts of the large metropolitan areas. But the growth will be so huge that new office-oriented subcenters will develop in the major metropolitan areas, housing functions that do not need to be downtown, but which find advantages in clustering together.

Most of these subcenters will be in suburban areas, or in smaller cities near what is now the periphery of the large metropolitan areas. However, there is a real potential for developing such subcenters in the outer parts of the central cities themselves. The larger central cities do have commercial subcenters outside their central business districts. Usually, they are places with good transportation connections, developed as commercial districts with department store branches and other shopping facilities to serve the surrounding population in a pre-automobile age. They, like the central business districts of smaller metropolitan areas within the orbit of the very largest ones, are natural growth points for the office-oriented subcenters of the future.

In most cases, this will occur only if concerted efforts are made with public intervention to acquire land, make long-range plans, and exercise leadership. But the possibility of

---

3. Regina Belz Armstrong, *The Office Industry: Patterns of Growth and Location,* a report of the Regional Plan Association (Cambridge, Mass.: The M.I.T. Press, 1972), p. 20.

developing centers housing as many as 30,000 jobs is a very real one. If the potential is realized, the gray areas surrounding the centers will possess great attractions as residential locations, in view of their accessibility to job sites. It would be reasonable to anticipate extensive private investment in housing in such areas—high-density housing closest to the centers themselves and lower-density housing further away, thus repeating the historic pattern of city development around the old central business districts. This then would be a form of gray-area redevelopment that involves a maximum of private investment and initiative and that adds to, rather than drains, central-city fiscal resources.

Development Patterns in Metropolitan Areas

The centers strategy has attractions for the future development of urban areas outside the central city, as well. A deliberate policy to foster the growth of relatively large subcenters can be a powerful tool to counter most of the undesirable consequences of the pattern of urban development that prevails in most metropolitan areas today.

Most of the increase in the American population has been occurring within metropolitan areas, but outside the central cities. By 1985, the population in the suburban ring will be nearly 50 million more than it was in 1966, but the central cities will increase by only about 6 million.[4] This is less than their expected natural increase—the excess of births over deaths—so that there will be net migration from cities to suburbs, as there has been since 1950.

---

4. See Patricia Leavey Hodge and Philip M. Hauser, *The Challenge of America's Metropolitan Population Outlook—1960 to 1985* (Washington, D.C.: National Commission on Urban Problems, 1968), Chap. 2.

Thus, decentralization and outward movement of the urban population is inevitable. But the form that this decentralization takes is not preordained. One would hope not, for there are some major disadvantages in the form that has been characteristic. That form has been characterized as "spread city,"[5] a type of development that is neither city nor country, with the advantages of neither: housing developed at uniform low densities, with larger and larger lot-sizes, plus commercial facilities, industrial plants, colleges, hospitals, and governmental offices scattered over the landscape virtually at random.

Among the disadvantages of "spread city" is its profligate consumption of land for low-density housing and for the vast parking fields required by each of many separately sited facilities, none of which are able to share parking lots with other facilities (as they might, if they were developed together). This pushes back the boundaries of the truly rural area and makes natural open space ever more distant. Most suburban settlers feel that they are moving to a more countrylike environment, but they do not find it. Large individual lots do not substitute for natural open space, in this sense, if indeed in any sense.

Perhaps more serious is the limitation on housing choice in such a pattern of development. Only one type of housing is available, the single-family detached house on a large lot, increasingly distant from the center of the metropolitan area. No doubt most families do prefer to live in single-family houses on relatively spacious sites. They surely do not all prefer to live where long journeys to work are necessary. Nor can

---

5. In *Spread City, Projections of Development Trends and the Issues They Pose: The Tri-State New York Metropolitan Region, 1960–1985* (New York: Regional Plan Association, 1962).

they all afford the higher purchase price that uniform large-lot zoning produces: in the late 1960s in northeastern metropolitan areas new houses on one-acre lots typically cost $5,000 more than identical new houses on 7,500-square-foot lots (one-sixth of an acre).

TABLE 5-1 *Illustration of Effects of Limits on Housing Choice*

| | Suburban Row Houses and Garden Apartments | Equivalent-Size Single-Family Houses | |
		7,500-Square-Foot Lots	One-Acre Lots
Selling Price[a]	$16,000	$21,500[b]	$26,500[c]
Approximate Monthly Cash Outlays Required[d]	155	210	255
Approximate Income Needed, If Housing Costs Are No More Than 25 Percent of Income	7,450	10,050	12,250

[a]Based on costs in large northeastern metropolitan areas from newspaper real estate advertising in the 1966-1968 period.

[b]Construction costs 30 percent above those for row houses and garden apartments; land costs about $1,000 higher.

[c]Land costs $5,000 more than for 7,500-square-foot lots.

[d]Includes mortgage payments on 30 year, 6.5 percent mortgage and annual costs for taxes, insurance, and heating at 5 percent of purchase price.

Moreover, single-family detached houses are not the cheapest type of housing to construct. In the suburban parts of the larger metropolitan areas, single-family detached houses cost about 30 percent more per square foot to build than two-story row houses and garden apartments of frame-and-brick construction. The latter can be highly attractive, but many suburban communities do not permit their construction. The effects of large-lot zoning and prohibition of the least expensive forms of construction are illustrated in Table 5-1, with data for the 1966–1968 period. A family with an income of $7,450 could have afforded a row house, with its monthly costs of $155.[6] But it would have taken an income of over $12,000 to afford a detached single-family house, of equal square-footage, on a one-acre lot.

This has serious implications for racial separation in metropolitan areas. No matter how effective antidiscrimination laws may be, most minority-group families are still barred from suburban areas, by the high price of suburban housing. Rowhouse construction could open these areas to moderate-income black families; with even modest subsidy, via the federal housing programs discussed in Chapter 4, the prices of such housing could be reduced to the point where considerably more than half of all black families in metropolitan areas could afford to live in suburban communities. This would permit far more rapid improvement in the housing conditions of the urban minority groups than any other strategy. Equally important, it would dramatically improve their access to the expanding job opportunities that exist in suburban areas.

Other disadvantages ascribed to "spread city" are the lack of sense of community on the part of its residents, for there is no central place with which to identify, and the lack of access to many urban-type facilities. Such facilities are scattered; many simply do not exist in suburbs because the necessary clientele for them is too dispersed. For example, studies of museum audiences have found that they consist heavily of nearby city residents; people apparently will not travel long distances to visit museums. As a result, there are a dozen American metropolitan areas with more than a million suburban residents, but no suburban museums. It may be that those who choose suburban living have no particular desire to enjoy museums and similar attractions; but even if they do have such desires, they have little opportunity to gratify them.

_____

6. In 1966, the median income of families in metropolitan areas was $8,200.

The "spread city" pattern does not produce urbanity in physical appearance. Its hallmarks are roadside commercial "ribbon" development, vast parking fields, and little variation in building height, size, and texture, because of the prevailing uniformity in building type. Again, this may be of slight concern to suburban residents, but with rising incomes and educational attainment there is evidence that concern with the appearance of the physical environment is increasingly widespread.

Finally, "spread city" leads to high transportation and utility costs. The dispersed pattern requires people to travel longer distances to work and to the scattered nonwork destinations;[7] utility lines must be run over longer distances. Moreover, there is a good deal of unanticipated congestion. The first plant or shopping center in a section may locate there in part because the roads are not congested. As others follow in unplanned sequence, congestion develops that might have been avoided with advance planning.

The centers strategy can eliminate many of these disadvantages. If offices, shopping, college campuses, hospitals, and cultural facilities are clustered in relatively large planned centers, each will build up a clientele for the others. They can be planned to utilize common supporting facilities, like parking, and to encourage architectural distinction. The effects on

---

7. It has been estimated that, if all work places are centralized, trip lengths from home to job increase with the square root of the increase in land area per dwelling; see Kent T. Healey, "Some Major Aspects of Urban Transport Policy Formation," in *Transportation Economics,* Universities–National Bureau Conference (New York: Columbia University Press, 1965), pp. 327–345. In 1970, the land area per occupied housing unit in American metropolitan areas with populations over 200,000 was 4.8 acres. If the average trip to work is 5 miles, an increase in land per dwelling to 6 acres would increase average trip lengths to 5.6 miles, according to the Healey formula.

housing patterns are equally important. If the centers are successful, they will inevitably lead to construction of apartments
right in the centers, occupied partly by those who work in the
centers; demand for such housing expressed through market
forces will do this almost automatically. Similarly, there will
be market pressure for medium-density housing, such as garden apartments, nearby. Densities can be expected to decrease
as the distance from the centers increases, with the more remote sections being occupied by very low-density, almost
rural, housing developments.

Logically, the centers would be located at points of maximum transportation advantage—near freeway interchanges or
at points of access to a suburban rail system, if it exists. The
concentration and high internal residential densities would
afford another transportation advantage: it would permit them
to serve as hubs for local bus service, which is usually exceedingly limited under "spread city" conditions.

Development of centers requires a deliberate policy of encouraging the clustering of facilities that might otherwise be
scattered in suburban areas. It was noted earlier that office
activities do tend to cluster. For other activities, three types of
public actions are required: coordination of decisions of public agencies on the location of public and quasi-public facilities
like colleges and hospitals; adjustment of already planned
transportation facilities, like freeways, to serve the centers;
and revision of land-use controls to permit land to be developed in the required ways.

It should be kept in mind that the diverse agencies that are
responsible for determining the location of new public facilities, like freeways, hospitals, and colleges, seldom make their
investment decisions in full recognition of the real interde-
pendence that exists. Often, the overriding criterion is land
costs; clearly, sites are cheaper the *further* they are from other

activities. This promotes scattering, not clustering. But this is surely a money illusion, the making of decisions on the basis of immediate money costs rather than on the basis of an analysis of long-term resource costs and benefits to the society as a whole, not just the individual public agency. Failure to make decisions on such broad grounds is, of course, a repudiation of the whole notion of public stewardship. Government agencies exist, not to minimize their own costs (or make life more tranquil for officials), but to maximize net benefits for the communities they serve.

By and large, the centers will be developed by permitting market forces to work: permitting offices to cluster as they seem to prefer and permitting higher-density housing attracted by the concentrations of activity to be built there. This is in sharp contrast to earlier notions about dealing with the disadvantages of "spread city." These involved efforts to concentrate industry in industrial parks. This is fine for smaller plants, but most large plants need separate locations, simply because of their vast size. There also were efforts to encourage higher residential densities on scattered tracts, but these efforts too were often bucking market forces rather than working with them.

The centers strategy can be considered an extension of the "new towns" approach, first advanced over twenty-five years ago in Britain. The idea in Britain was to relieve overcrowded large cities like London by "decanting" some of their population into self-contained new towns beyond the economic pull of the large city, towns complete with jobs for all their residents. There is an inherent weakness in this approach, in that the self-contained new town tends to be relatively small (thus making only a small contribution to the accommodation of a growing urban population). This is because the new town is so far from the metropolitan center and because the local market for its own services, ranging from retail stores to the provision of job opportunities, is initially a small one.

The American variant of new towns, places like Columbia in Maryland, is rather different. Instead of distant, self-contained communities, there is large-scale development of new communities on the fringes of large metropolitan areas, but within easy reach of them. Such communities can capitalize on their proximity to both the metropolitan central business district and the large existing suburban population, providing the latter with jobs and services as well as new housing choices. Like the British new towns, the American ones contain industry and office activities, but it is anticipated that many of those living in the new towns will work elsewhere, many in the central city. And many of those working in the new towns will not live there. The new towns, however, will be centers with varied economic activities, cultural facilities, and housing densities, in short, the kinds of centers discussed here. But not all centers need be wholly new towns developed by a single entrepreneur. Others could be expansions and re-developments of existing outlying towns and small cities, which already possess on a small scale many of the attributes of the large-scale centers.

Controlling Land Uses

The centers strategy involves two types of policy instruments. First, there is the deliberate and systematic use, in an entrepreneurial manner, of the power to decide where new public facilities should be located. Second, there is adjustment of the rules governing private decision making on land uses, in large part to allow the market forces to work themselves out. Ours is a society that necessarily involves a great deal of decentralized decision making by private individuals, voluntary associations, and local governments; this decision making takes place under general rules, with financial incentives and deterrents, like taxes, subsidies, and grants, added to influence decision makers.

However, in land uses, the basic instrument that sets rules within which private decisions must be made—zoning—is not general, but highly specific. Moreover, it is not continuous, like taxes or subsidies (a more expensive building attracts higher property taxes; building additional public housing units attracts more federal grants). Instead, zoning is a yes-or-no control: either the land use is permitted or it is prohibited. There is a third, equally drastic, alternative: public purchase of the land in question.

In planning for land use in urban areas, governments perform two roles.[8] First, there is a forecasting role. Neither public nor private land-use decisions can be sensibly made without some assumption about the future use of other land in the vicinity. Public planners, by forecasting expected changes in land use as far ahead as possible, can help improve the decisions made by private land users and by public agencies investing in new facilities. A second role is to control specific private land-use decisions.

A yes-or-no control system like zoning can be justified only if it is believed that the forecasts provide for so nearly an optimal pattern of land use that they must be adhered to rigidly, and if it is believed that community interests and private interests will be in conflict frequently. Otherwise, a system of controls that allowed more flexibility in land-use decision making would clearly be preferable. But it should be obvious

---

8. A good discussion of this, reflected in part in the following paragraphs, can be found in Max Neutze, *The Suburban Apartment Boom* (Washington, D.C.: Resources for the Future, 1968), pp. 127–137, 148–150.

that no planning agency making long-range forecasts can be omniscient; therefore deviations from the plan are likely to be desirable on many occasions. Also, the community and private land users are often not in head-on conflict. For example, the community might be marginally better off if a proposed building covered less of its site than the builder proposes, but the builder's proposal, if effected, will not be catastrophic. An ideal control system would offer the builder incentives for lower site coverage, rather than prohibit higher site coverage outright.

There are two such ideal control systems that might be used. One would be public ownership of *all* urban land and its lease for relatively short periods, like twenty years. The short leases would permit changes in land uses over time, as leases expired. More importantly, the ground rent could be used as the instrument of control, by charging somewhat higher ground rents for marginally less attractive land uses and very much higher ground rents for even less attractive land uses. This would compel public agencies controlling land use to answer the following question: just how bad, in quantitative terms, is the private developer's proposal? If it is deemed bad simply because it raises costs of providing public services, the proposal could be accepted if the developer were willing to pay a ground rent high enough to defray the extra public costs.

A second system, of a type economists tend to prefer, permits private land ownership, but instead imposes variable taxes and subsidies on different land uses. The marginally less attractive land use is subject to a higher tax; the most attractive land uses can be offered outright subsidies. As the community develops, the tax and subsidy terms can be changed to encourage more (or discourage less) specific land uses.

One major advantage of the system is that it offers the private developer an opportunity to make adjustments in his plan to get better financial terms, if these better terms are worthwhile. Moreover, he can trade off among the various features of his proposal to get the best terms. For example, he might provide more off-street parking in order to be permitted greater site coverage. To be sure, some existing zoning ordinances, such as those in Chicago and New York, have trade-off provisions, but they are far more clumsy instruments than would be possible under a system of variable taxes and subsidies.

Another advantage of such a system is that it could provide for direct monetary compensation to owners of adjacent land for damages a proposed new land use might do to them. Zoning is designed to limit such damages, but the only option an adjacent land user has is to fight the proposed new use, no matter how small the prospective harm. For example, higher-density housing in a neighborhood might increase traffic volumes. Even if the increase is a small one, there is an incentive to object to the proposed zoning change. But there are many cases in which payments of financial damages, for example, enabling existing property owners to put up protective fences and shrubbery, might be sufficient to eliminate the objection.

Clearly, such a system requires a great deal of sophisticated decision making by planning agencies, in explicit, quantitative terms. It is by no means easy to implement. But the difficulties should not disqualify the approach. It should be kept in mind that the existing control system—zoning—does involve public decision making on the same issues. However, the weighting of the factors involved is implicit rather than explicit and the whole process is surrounded by a cloud of legal fictions. The legal question asked is this one: does the proposed land use endanger the public health, safety, and morals? Because the answer is almost always no, if these terms are defined by their dictionary meanings, a whole array of legal definitions and subterfuges have emerged since zoning was first instituted a half century ago. But, surely, explicit, rather than implicit, public decision making is preferable, and straightforward answers are preferable to legal dodges.

Explicit, quantitative analysis of costs and benefits also seems to be the superior way of handling the many conflicts in land uses that are not now resolved by zoning. In nearly every major urban area, there are increasing conflicts centering on parks and other open space, aesthetics (including preservation of historic buildings and districts), and uses of waterfront land. It was suggested in Chapter 2 that these conflicts are partly a consequence of increasing urbanization, but more often they are a reflection of the realization that a rich society need not accept nineteenth-century standards of urban amenity. We *can* afford to withhold urban land from other uses, including highways, for parks and open space; we *can* afford the frequently higher costs of more attractive new structures or preservation of somewhat inefficient older ones that are highly attractive; and we *can* afford to "return waterfronts to people," by removing old commercial and industrial uses that developed a century ago.

Typically, the problem is that while the benefits from such land uses are very considerable, they are general and diffused. In contrast, the higher costs are specific and concentrated: the highway agency must stretch its appropriation to buy privately owned land rather than run the road through a park; or it must spend additional amounts to avoid building an elevated expressway that would blight a highly attractive place, like Jackson Square in the Vieux Carré in New Orleans; or a private owner must remodel an existing building in a historic district, like Georgetown in Washington, Beacon Hill in Boston, Brooklyn Heights in New York, or the Vieux Carré, instead of building an efficient new high-rise structure. Those confronted with the higher costs naturally resist, and often are successful.

The needs are threefold. First, there is need for comprehensive analyses of social, as well as private, costs and benefits. Second, there is need for governmental instrumentalities to make these analyses and implement their findings. The growing use of systems analysis in governments, at all levels, can help on this score. Third, there is need for adequate compensation of the losers from this process and, simultaneously, for incentives to public and private land users to make the right choices. For example, if public agencies, like highway departments, had to make payments in lieu of taxes on the land they use (and make higher payments where the land use is incompatible with adjacent land uses, as at Jackson Square in New Orleans), they might well make very different decisions.

6

The Quality of the
Urban Environment

In the broadest sense, the quality of the urban environment is determined by a very wide array of conditions and policies, including those that bear on the attractiveness of the buildings we use and see daily, the character and use of both open and developed land, and the ease of access to destinations that are attractive, as well as the cleanliness of water, air, and land surfaces. Some of these conditions and policies have been considered in the preceding two chapters on housing and land use; others will be considered in the following chapter on transportation. In this chapter, we focus on policies that deal with those assaults on the quality of the environment resulting from air and water pollution, which is what most people now mean when they express concern about environmental quality. However, it is worth noting that pollution and congestion have some marked economic similarities. Both are external *diseconomies,* in which individual decisions about fuels, industrial processes, goods consumed, and trips made may be reasonable from the individual's standpoint, but may impose costs on society as a whole. Both are much more serious problems under conditions of rising population size and

174

density, and hence in urban areas. In both types of situations, there are thresholds below which the external damages are minimal, but damages increase disproportionately once these thresholds are passed.[1]

Concerted public action to deal with pollution problems in large cities is by no means a wholly new thing. The downtown Pittsburgh "renaissance" of the 1950s was founded on elimination of the air pollution caused by the burning of bituminous coal that had given Pittsburgh an international reputation as the "Smoky City." Comprehensive planning for sewage treatment in urban areas dates back at least as far as the 1890s, when court orders resulted in creation of the Chicago Sanitary District and reversal of the flow of the Chicago River. However, pollution remained the most unglamorous of public issues, with proposed public actions shaped largely by considerations of engineering efficiency, but limited by the political infeasibility of costly actions to deal with what was then a low-priority concern.

The new concern with pollution has led to a new language to describe its essential nature. One example is the term "materials balance," which describes the self-contained, closed system that our planet is; the quantity of materials placed into the productive process is withdrawn from the environment and will in time be returned to the environment in one form or another, less materials that have been recycled (waste or scrap). In 1965, the productive process in the United States withdrew roughly 2.5 billion tons of active materials (that is, excluding inactive materials like sand and gravel used in construction that present no real disposal problems) from the

---

1. See Jerome Rothenberg, "The Economics of Congestion and Pollution: An Integrated View," *American Economic Review* 60 (May 1970): 114–121.

environment, about 10 percent in the form of food, another 10 percent in forest products, and somewhat over 50 percent in the form of mineral fuels.[2]

The environmental issues are threefold. First, how can the environmental damages done in the process of withdrawing some of these materials—like strip mining of coal and clear cutting of timber—be minimized? Although this issue is of concern to all of us, the location of the problem is rural, not urban, and it will not be considered further here. Second, how much can the magnitude of the disposal problem be reduced by increased recycling of materials? Third, how much can the disposal problem be reduced by changing the *forms* in which waste materials are discharged? There is a considerable degree of possible substitutability in waste discharge form. A mundane example is kitchen garbage, which is solid waste with one set of collection and disposal problems if placed into a garbage can and liquid waste with other problems if ground up in a kitchen-sink disposal unit.

The mix of wastes discharged into the environment depends upon the technology of production at a given time, the cost and availability of inputs that can substitute for one another (like different fuels), the mix of goods actually produced—for here the range of substitution is very wide indeed —the environmental damages done by different waste discharges, and the cost or penalties attached to each of the discharges. An important concept here is the assimilative or absorptive capacity of the environment—how much waste the natural environment can absorb before any damages become discernible. A swiftly flowing stream, for example, dilutes all wastes, degrades some inorganic wastes, and re-

---

2. Robert Ayres and Allen Kneese, "Environmental Pollution," in *Federal Programs for the Development of Human Resources,* vol. 2, (Washington, D.C.: Joint Economic Committee, U. S. Congress, 1968), p. 630.

stores the dissolved oxygen demanded of it by limited amounts of organic wastes; a zero level of discharges is really not necessary to preserve environmental quality. But as the assimilative capacity of the natural environment is approached, the incremental damages done by additional waste discharges become increasingly apparent and increasingly objectionable. In urban areas, where people, activities, and the generation of wastes are spatially concentrated, the assimilative capacity of the natural environment is least equal to the demands placed upon it.

Therefore, pollution as an external diseconomy is worst in urban areas. Individual producers and consumers keep their own costs low by not trying to minimize the quantity or harmfulness of the wastes they generate and discharge. The price for this is deterioration in environmental quality, but that price traditionally has not been reflected in the decisions made by producers and consumers. Another way of putting it is that a high-quality environment—pure air and water—is valuable, but it is not sold in the market. Instead, it is a "common property right," available to all at a zero price. Not surprisingly, the environment is overloaded, and too few resources are devoted to protection of the environment.

Pollution as an Economic Problem

Although the technical characteristics of pollution and of policies to reduce it are matters for engineers and physical scientists, the pollution problem is essentially an economic one. It arises because individual producers and consumers are presented with improper economic signals—the wrong structure of rewards and penalties—in the absence of the right kind of public intervention. But what is the right kind of intervention?

A fundamental issue here concerns the standards of environmental quality to be pursued. If zero pollution could be achieved at no cost at all, this would be the appropriate solution. But it is clear that reducing pollution has substantial resource costs, and the evidence is compelling that the costs of pollution removal rise very steeply as the standards of environmental quality rise. For example, it is typically more than five times as costly, per unit of additional pollutant removed, to remove 95 percent of the most common polluting effect of organic wastes in water (biochemical oxygen demand, or BOD) as it is to remove 40 percent of the pollutant.[3]

In the past, standards, or rather aspirations, have come from what has been called the "requirements" approach. Engineers, planners, or other experts define requirements in some absolute physical terms, independent of the costs of achieving these requirements and without any precise measurement of the benefits to be realized by one particular standard as compared to another. Thus, we are told, for example, that sewage must be treated to remove x percent of the BOD in raw sewage. Clearly, lower standards may be satisfactory under some conditions and higher ones desirable under others. The purity of water necessary for swimming, for drinking, and for recreational boating differs greatly, and there are large differences in the costs of attaining these differing degrees of purity. It is by no means clear that the net social benefits of making *all* water courses pure enough for swimming are greater than, say, having lower standards of water quality and building more swimming pools supplied with heavily treated water, but away from any river or lake.

---

3. Ivars Gutmanis, "The Generation and Cost of Controlling Air, Water and Solid Waste Pollution: 1970–2000," an analysis prepared for The Brookings Institution (April 1972; processed).

Absolute standards for any form of pollution are inherently unreasonable, for they are likely to impose large costs on some sectors and yield smaller net social benefits than a more discriminating set of standards. One aspect of this is discrimination among those generating a given type of pollutant. The traditional form of water-pollution-control policy is to require each industrial polluter and municipal water treatment plant to reduce pollution (measured in BOD) by a uniform percentage. But the costs of doing this vary greatly among individual sources of effluent (as do the benefits from such a policy, as noted above). The least-cost approach for achieving any given overall environmental quality target requires that each firm or municipal plant remove wastes to the point where the cost of removing an additional pound is the same as that for every other source of pollution. This rule, as the reader can see, is strikingly similar to the more general conditions for realizing Pareto-efficiency in resource allocation, which was discussed in Chapter 1.

A number of studies show that the total costs of achieving a given target via the uniform-reduction approach can be 1.5, 2, or even 3 times more than the least-cost approach. Moreover, the uniform-reduction approach does not allow for the possibilities of reducing damage by substituting raw materials that are less polluting, in the course of the production process (for example, using more scrap and less virgin ore in metal smelting), or by producing products that contribute less to pollution (for example, unbleached household paper products can be produced with far less water pollution than bleached paper).

A second major issue is the inadequacy of the governmental machinery for applying controls and for supplying the needed environmental services in urban areas. Traditionally, the quality of the environment in the United States has been the concern of local governments. Within urban areas, actions to control water and air pollution and disposal of solid waste are largely carried out by municipal governments, each covering only a small part of the total metropolitan area. True, there are a few area-wide sewerage agencies, but by and large these activities are handled by governmental agencies with narrow geographic scope.

The problems, however, spill over municipal boundaries and cover whole metropolitan areas or even larger regions, like water basins, and small-area governments are entirely inadequate to deal with such problems. In some cases, it is physically impossible to provide the necessary service. A small municipality cannot ensure that the air its residents breathe is unpolluted, for neighboring communities may be the source of the air pollution.

In other cases, like water pollution, there is a different kind of externality. One city's water may be pure enough, but it can pollute the water supply of its downstream neighbors by inadequately treating its sewage. The upstream city has no incentive to tax its own residents to purify water for others, and to expect it to do so, in the absence of compulsion, is to expect people to be far more philanthropic than ordinary taxpayers are. Therefore, there has been increasing state government and federal government intervention. The intervention of the larger government makes it possible to internalize the external costs; that is, the costs of pollution imposed on others are external to the polluting city, but internal to the state or to the nation as a whole. The larger governments intervene in two ways, with both carrot and stick. They offer grants to local governments to improve sewage treatment, and they compel municipalities and industrial polluters to apply higher standards of water treatment and air quality.

By now there is general agreement that it is essential that the federal government set minimum standards for air and water quality, although there is less agreement about the standards themselves, about whether states and localities should be permitted to set even higher standards, and about how the standards should be enforced. A major argument for federal minimum standards is the reasonable fear that individual states might set low standards in order to attract pollution-prone industry from places that attempt to enforce high ·environmental standards and that, as a defensive measure, the high-standard states then would relax their enforcement efforts.

At present, the disposal of solid wastes is even more a matter for small-area local governments than is the disposal of liquid or gaseous wastes. There are virtually no metropolitan-area-wide or regional agencies and no state or federal intervention. Yet, the problem is a growing one; solid wastes are generated at the rate of nearly one ton per capita annually in urban areas now and this rate may very well double by the year 2000. It is a regional problem, because the predominant disposal method is land fill (that is, dumping), and available land-fill sites in the closer-in parts of metropolitan areas are rapidly being exhausted. An alternative disposal method is incineration or on-site burning, but most municipal and private incinerators (as well as backyard burning of refuse) contribute heavily to air pollution.

This illustrates the interaction among environmental quality programs. In the late 1960s for example, New York City adopted a rigorous set of air-quality controls that required the closing down of some municipal incinerators and the closing down or upgrading of private incinerators in apartment houses. The result was a massive increase in the garbage collection and disposal load, so massive that air-polluting incinerators have been permitted to continue in operation, despite the law.

Thus, the waste management aspects of dealing with environmental quality appear to require some major changes in governmental machinery.[4] One is the creation of regional agencies to deal with this truly regional problem and to achieve economies of large-scale operation in new incineration methods and sewage disposal plants. A second is to handle the partly interchangeable forms of waste—solid, liquid and gaseous—jointly rather than separately.

Beyond this, there is need for much more knowledge about the damages caused by pollution; we really do not know how much it is worth to eliminate a particular waste, and so we spend a great deal to eliminate some wastes that may not be very damaging, while not doing enough to eliminate really damaging wastes. Moreover, there has been too little research on new methods of handling wastes, such as long-distance shipment of compacted solid wastes to ocean disposal sites or abandoned strip mines; similarly, there is need for research on the possibilities of using materials, for example in packaging, that decompose more readily.

The lack of knowledge and the inadequacy of the research efforts are direct consequences of the cumbersome governmental machinery: no single city has the incentive or resources to invest in research that will benefit all cities. Indeed, the incentive here is really nationwide, not just regional. Only the federal government is really equipped to internalize the benefits from much greater research efforts. The situation is strikingly similar to that of health research twenty years ago; there was relatively little federal support. Awareness of the nationwide benefits has led to our acceptance today of the fact that

---

4. One of the best comprehensive studies of the problem, done for the New York area, is *Waste Management* (New York: Regional Plan Association, 1968).

health research is, and must be, largely a federal responsibility.

Regulation versus Charges

A third issue concerns the methods that should be used in controlling pollution, given appropriate standards and governmental machinery.

As in the case of land-use controls, the control system ordinarily used in waste management is a yes-or-no system: actions are either prohibited or permitted. As with land use, there is good reason to employ a variant of the price system—variable charges on the generation of wastes. Sewage charges related to the quality and volume of effluent have been used in the Ruhr Basin in Germany for many years, but sewer service charges in America, where they are used (they are by no means universal), are usually related only to the volume of water intake. In theory, a governmental regulatory agency could apply a variable standard, seeking to reduce pollution where the costs are least, by setting pollution limits individually for each and every source of pollution. However, this would be a staggering and impossible administrative burden, requiring knowledge of changing costs, technological possibilities, input alternatives, and output mixes for hundreds of thousands of pollution sources.

A system of charges can overcome this. Faced with variable charges, each polluting establishment would find it in its own interest to reduce waste generation by amounts that depend upon the cost of reduction and also to find the least costly way of achieving the reduction. Moreover, if polluters are taxed for each unit of pollution, they will not stop trying to reduce pollution when they reach some specified standard: it can pay them to reduce pollution even further. This is highly important, because continued economic growth requires that individual polluters do an increasingly good job of reducing waste generation.

In short, there are a number of strong arguments for variable charges on pollutants. One is that we simply do not know enough either about the damages done by given quantities of a given pollutant or about the costs of reducing pollution emissions from individual sources to be able to set appropriate across-the-board prohibitions. What we do know is that the costs of control vary a good deal and rise with rising environmental standards. Effluent charges would shift the economizing decisions to the polluters themselves and would significantly reduce the emissions of pollutants we are unable or unwilling to prohibit outright.

A second argument for charges, this time for geographically variable ones, relates to the location of the sources of wastes. There are some locations outside urban areas where industrial plants can emit noxious gases or liquid effluents with lesser social damage, because the assimilative capacity of the natural environment is relatively greater. If the waste charges are low in such places and high in densely populated urban areas, such plants may very well move to the isolated places; if they do, this suggests that the really optimal location for them, from an overall social standpoint, is not in the urban areas.

A third argument relates to the location of the disposal process. Some wastes might be disposed of more efficiently at the place they are produced—in the home or factory. But such cost comparisons simply will not be made unless the costs of external waste disposal are reflected in the charges that must be paid. Yet another argument is that charges can actually reduce the volume of waste created, where it is not possible to prohibit wastes—for example, waste charges on beverage manufacturers might induce them to find ways to develop decomposable containers; a close cost calculation might even suggest a return to reusable glass containers rather than no-return bottles and cans.

In short, the objective of charges is to confront private decision makers with the social costs of their decisions and thereby provide them with incentives to come to different decisions. Charges do not obviate the need for better knowledge and still less for better governmental organization to deal with environmental quality. But in a world of imperfect knowledge and inadequate machinery, a system of charges instead of yes-or-no controls is likely to produce fewer major mistakes and will be amenable to more frequent adjustment. This, at least, is the economist's argument. The decisions regarding the allocation of resources for the 70 percent of the gross national product (GNP) that is produced in the private sector of the economy are largely made on the basis of the prices confronting the individual and business decision makers. These decisions seem to work out a good deal better than do our decisions on environmental quality, where the pricing system is largely ignored or gives the wrong signals.

Because the forms of pollution are so varied, the charging devices to deal with them should take a number of different forms. For water pollution, the most frequently proposed form of effluent charge is one measured by pounds of BOD discharged. An often cited figure is a charge of 8 or 10 cents a pound. For the average polluter, the marginal cost of removing a pound of BOD at the 90 percent removal level may well be about 10 cents. Thus, such a charge would make an overall removal level of 90 percent in a river basin financially advantageous. Polluters with higher costs would remove a lesser percentage, but those with lower costs would remove more. All of them would have an incentive to find new low-cost ways to reduce **BOD** discharges, by new technology, internal control devices, and changes in product mix (for example, by switching to the output of unbleached paper products). The charge could be set at a low level initially, increasing each year to allow control measures to be put into operation.

One possible way of dealing with one of more serious air-pollution problems, sulfur emissions, was proposed by the Nixon Administration in 1972: a graduated tax on sulfur emissions, a tax highest in airsheds with the poorest air quality and zero in airsheds with acceptable air quality from the standpoint of sulfur emissions. An analogous approach to automotive emissions might be to impose a tax on each make of new car, graduated according to its pollution emissions.

Most other pollution tax proposals are designed not to improve pollution-control performance by polluters themselves, but to reduce or eliminate use of products that are objectionable on environmental grounds. These include the proposed tax on leaded gasoline designed to eliminate the production of leaded gasoline entirely in time; taxes on the quantity of packaging materials, with adjustments for recycling of materials, designed to reduce the generation of solid wastes; increased taxes on auto use designed simply to reduce the volume of traffic; and special taxes on new cars, refundable to the final owner if he disposes of the car in an approved manner, rather than abandoning it in the streets or on public property.

Some people object to effluent charges, saying that they are in fact "licenses to pollute," because the polluter who pays the charge is no longer committing an illegal act by discharging wastes. But there is a license to pollute in the setting of any limit on pollution above zero. Effluent charges can be set to yield any level of environmental purity we wish to achieve. The difference is that, with charges, there will indeed be legal variations in the volume of pollutants emitted from different sources; with regulation, such variations will be illegal, and some of the violators will be punished. The more effective the enforcement effort, the greater the enforcement costs will be. This too makes regulation anything but a least-cost solution.

There is another, wholly different approach to controlling pollution that has had some recent popularity: stopping or drastically reducing economic growth. It is true that, now that the rate of population growth in the United States has slowed considerably, the principal source of increased waste generation in the future will be increased per capita use of materials. Because there are ultimate limits on overall planetary material use, why not try to anticipate what will be necessary ultimately by slowing economic growth here and now? One reply, which is not really relevant to the pollution argument, is that this is morally indefensible in that rapid overall economic growth is the only effective means any society has found to truly improve the living standards of its poorer people.

A second reply is more to the point: in the United States, economic growth to some extent does, and increasingly can, take forms that are less materials using: that is, an increasing share of consumption can be of services that use much labor and long-lived capital, rather than goods and services that require heavy inputs of materials that are quickly returned to the environment. Appropriate pollution-control policies would encourage this significantly. For example, the principal additional resource input needed if returnable beverage containers were generally used would be labor; returnable containers were abandoned because labor is expensive, whereas materials—in the absence of appropriate taxes and charges—have been cheap.

Finally, for the immediate future, economic growth in the United States can be consistent with a major improvement in environmental quality. The annual costs in 1980 of achieving

very high standards of air and water quality have been estimated at no more than $100 billion.[5] This would be a massive
program, but at a 4 percent real annual growth rate, GNP in
1980 would be $425 billion greater than in 1972. Thus, the
nation could achieve both high environmental quality and
increased living standards simultaneously, by devoting less
than one-fourth of the increase in GNP to pollution control.
Stopping economic growth to achieve a better environment
seems both unnecessary and unwise at this point in the world's
history, although it surely will be necessary some day. If
irreversible environmental damages can be prevented by public action here and now—and there is every reason to believe
that this is entirely possible—and if overall environmental
quality can be improved while economic growth continues for
decades, or even a century or more, ahead, we would be be-
having irresponsibly to our immediate posterity (the next two
or three generations) to call a halt to growth many years
before it is truly necessary. We must consider the future, to be
sure, but the fact of our own mortality and the lack of cer-
tainty in forecasting for the very distant future require that
we heavily discount the prospects of ecological disaster hundreds or even thousands of years from now.

---

5. See Charles L. Schultze, Edward R. Fried, Alice M. Rivlin, and Nancy H.
Teeters, *Setting National Priorities: The 1973 Budget* (Washington, D.C.:
The Brookings Institution, 1972), pp. 373–375. Their chapter on the environment is one of the best concise treatments of the subject and is the
source of some of the ideas advanced here.

7

Transportation

The really big issue in urban transportation policy for at least a decade has been the controversy about how much emphasis to place on new investment in urban highways vis-à-vis improvements in public transportation facilities and services. This controversy is founded on disagreement over a number of underlying issues, including the effects (if any) of transportation on the pattern of urban development; the role of apparent consumer preferences in determining transportation investment; the use of the price system; and the role of the different levels of government. But before examining these issues and the policies they imply, it is well to ask: are the two modes of "transportation (the private auto and public transportation) really as competitive as the heat of the controversy implies?

The Distinctive Roles of Transportation Modes

In American urban areas as a whole, travel in private automobiles accounts for roughly 95 percent of all travel (excluding pedestrian movement). In the aggregate, travel by bus, subway, suburban railroad, taxicab, and ferry appears rela-

189

tively unimportant, even in the very large metropolitan areas that have extensive transit, rail, and taxi services. This, however, refers to all kinds of urban travel, regardless of purpose of trip, location within the urban area, time of day or day of week. The urban transportation problem, however, can be more narrowly defined. Public policy is concerned with travel at the times and along the routes that involve congestion and needs for additional investment to improve service.

Much of the congestion problem is associated with journeys to work, because these tend to be concentrated into a few hours of each working day. Moreover, the worst of the journey-to-work congestion problem is connected with trips to and from the central business districts of large cities, because very large numbers of people are trying to move along a necessarily limited number of routes to or from a relatively confined geographic area, the central business district (CBD). There are, indeed, congestion problems connected with journeys to and from the growing number of non-CBD work places, especially when travel to and from them uses routes also used by CBD-bound travelers. But this class of congestion problems tends to be less severe, simply because the work places are more diffused throughout the urban area. Another secondary congestion problem is connected with summer and holiday weekend travel, especially in and around the very largest metropolitan areas.

In the largest urban areas, public transportation is relatively important in the journey to work. The New York region is the extreme case: there nearly half of the travel by some form of conveyance other than shanks' mare is public transportation rather than private automobile. For urban America as a whole, it appears that roughly 20 percent of all passenger-miles in journeys to work (excluding walking) is traveled by bus, subway, or suburban railroad (see Table 7-1). But over 99 percent of all other travel is by private automobile.

Thus, for all practical purposes, the auto and public transportation do not compete for the non-journey-to-work travel. True, there are some CBD shopping trips by public transportation in the largest cities, particularly in New York. Also, there is some nonwork usage of public transportation by people who lack access to cars: children, older people, people

TABLE 7-1 *Estimated Distribution of Urban Passenger-Miles by Mode and Type of Trip*[a]

	Bus, Subway, and Suburban Rail	Private Auto
All Types of Trips[b]	5%	95%
Journey to Work	20	80
Other Trips	1	99

[a]Estimated by author, largely on the basis of data in the *Statistical Abstract of the United States.* A "passenger-mile" is one passenger traveling one mile; thus, a five-mile trip by a car with two passengers equals ten passenger-miles and a three-mile trip by a bus with thirty passengers equals ninety passenger-miles. The data are as of 1970.

[b]Includes *only* transit, suburban rail, and private auto; excludes walking, taxi, ferry, and drivers and passengers in trucks.

with very low incomes. But the real competition is for journey-to-work trips, and this competition is by and large limited in two dimensions. It is limited to the rush hours at the beginning and end of the working day, and it is confined largely to CBD-oriented journey-to-work trips. Even for the journey to work, there are few public transportation trips that do not both occur in the peak hours and have one end of the trip in the CBD.

There are in effect three different urban transportation markets. One market comprises a relatively small number of people, typically central-city residents, who use public transportation for *all* the trips they take, a group defined by age, disability, or low income. A second market consists of CBD-oriented, mostly journey-to-work trips during peak hours by people who do, or could, have access to cars; here there is vigorous competition among the transport modes. The third market consists of everything else—trips that do not involve the CBD; trips during off-peak hours; trips not connected with travel to work. For such trips, the overwhelming preference is clearly for the private automobile.

This is not at all surprising. Indeed, it is almost inconceivable that public transportation could make much of a dent in this third market, no matter how good the service was or how low the fares were. For these trips, the automobile has great advantages in speed in nearly all cases. The frequency of service on public transportation is necessarily lower in off-peak hours and for non-CBD service; if trip origins and destinations are sufficiently dispersed, no public transportation service at all may be feasible. Finally, one major item of out-of-pocket cost for peak-hour, CBD-oriented, private auto trips, namely, downtown parking, is not a problem in this third market.

Although public transportation systems are designed largely for their main job, in the second market, all of them have a real interest in attracting more off-peak riders. Even a small addition to the number of off-peak riders can greatly improve the economic viability of public transportation, because there is little extra cost to the system in serving more riders during off-peak hours. But this must be viewed as no more than a minor by-product benefit, that improves the system's financial position and enables it better to serve its users in both the competitive second market and the captive first market.

The "Highway Bias" in Public Policy

Public policy thus is not necessarily biased in favor of the private auto and against public transportation, simply because of heavy governmental investment in highways in metropolitan areas. If there is a bias, it must be found in the transportation services and facilities offered in the second market, where the two modes truly compete. The frequent charge is that, within this market, the competition has not been on even terms. As noted in Chapter 2, this charge has two components. First, public policies have produced inappropriate systems of charging for the use of transportation services; second, the competing modes have had grossly unequal access to capital for new investment.

The system of charging for use can be evaluated only in the light of the way competing transport facilities are used. A public transportation system must recover most of its costs from charges imposed on those who ride in the peak periods, because there are relatively few other users. Some suburban railroads carry over 80 percent of their traffic in the predominant direction at peak hours; most transit systems carry half or more of their passengers during the peak hours. In contrast, a freeway system has its costs spread over a larger group, because the peaking characteristics of freeways are far less. There are few major freeways on which as much as a third of the traffic is accounted for by peak-hour, predominant-direction trips.

Superficially, this suggests that the freeway is likely to have a significant *inherent* price advantage over public transportation in the competition. There are simply more users of the system during nonpeak hours who can share the cost for the freeway system. But this is true only if one assumes that the appropriate pricing policy is the present one: uniform prices confronting all users regardless of the time of day or direction of travel and regardless of whether the travel is within or to the CBD or not.

Although the pricing policies do not distinguish between peak-hour and nonpeak travel, urban transportation planners do so in determining investment requirements and system design. Planners estimate the volumes of traffic that will present themselves to be served at the peak hours and try to build a system accordingly. The convention in highway planning is to design a system adequate to provide for the free flow of traffic (at some specified speed) at the demand expected in the thirtieth most busy hour during the year, a device designed to exclude the extremes of summer weekend and holiday travel, and thereby to accommodate peak-hour demand on a normal weekday. This estimate of demand for highways is made on the basis of the prevailing price system confronting users—that is, the cost of using the facility consists of the gasoline taxes that will be paid for that specific use, which are fairly nominal amounts. In effect, the demand is estimated as if the highway service were a free good.

In contrast, the transit user must pay *some* price, subsidized perhaps, but greater than zero. Transit planning, therefore, must assume that some people will be deterred from using the system by the fare. This difference between transit and highway planning tends to restrict investment in the former relative to the latter. However, this is not the most important difference related to pricing policies.

If, in fact, most transit usage is peak-hour usage, then even a uniform fare policy of the type that prevails in the United States is reasonably close to the appropriate price for peak-hour usage—a price reflecting the full costs of providing additional units of peak-hour service. Suppose it was decided to permit off-peak users to ride free, on the grounds that they impose no additional costs on the transit system—the crews, vehicles, rolling stock, tracks, stations, and so on, needed for rush-hour traffic are already on hand and paid for, whether or not people use them in off-peak hours. Suppose also that 80 percent of the users are peak-hour riders, as on some suburban rail systems. To cover system costs, fares paid by peak-hour riders would have to rise by 25 percent (100% = 80% × 1.25).

But the comparable rise in prices paid by peak-hour, CBD-oriented motorists, necessary if they too are to pay the full costs of their use of resources, would be vastly greater. Remember that highways *are* designed for rush-hour use, with extra lanes, ramps, traffic-control devices, and so on, that would not be needed to serve the smaller volumes of off-peak traffic. Another element of peak-hour marginal cost comes from the additional congestion created by extra users. When a highway is crowded to, or above, its designed capacity, each additional vehicle slows the flow of traffic further and makes the trip longer for all the users. Thus the full social cost of a peak-hour trip on a crowded highway would include an allowance for the value of the extra time lost by all other motorists. Failure to confront would-be users of private autos with these costs encourages people to use a means of transportation with very high resource costs; if they were confronted with the true costs, they might choose other alternatives.

There have been a number of estimates of the full social costs involved in peak-hour use of high-capacity urban freeways to and from the CBD. One such estimate is that the costs commonly exceed 11 cents per vehicle-mile.[1] Ordinarily, the only prices for specific trips on highways that motorists confront are the gasoline taxes they pay, taxes that amount to no more than 1 cent per vehicle-mile.[2] So the peak-hour motorist should really be paying a price for highway use which is ten (or more) times greater than the price he usually does pay,

1. See Lyle C. Fitch and Associates, *Urban Transportation and Public Policy* (San Francisco: Chandler, 1964), pp. 122–146, 265–266.
2. If the combined state and federal gasoline tax is 10 cents per gallon, the cost will be less than one cent per vehicle-mile unless the car gets less than 10 miles per gallon.

while the peak-hour transit rider's fare should rise by much smaller proportions.[3]

An extreme case—for example, the construction of a new subway line in New York City to relieve overcrowding—might require a threefold or fourfold increase in the transit rider's fare. For peak-hour motorists, the extreme cases are truly fantastic. For example, if peak-hour users of the proposed third tube of the Queens Midtown Tunnel in New York, required only for rush-hour traffic, had to pay its full costs, the indicated toll would be close to $10, compared to 50 cents at present (1973).

This is not to argue that urban highways in general are more heavily subsidized than transit systems. In fact, the opposite appears to be true. Gasoline taxes, vehicle taxes, tolls, and other charges collected from urban highway users are roughly equal to total public expenditure for urban highways, including highway-related police and court costs. In contrast, fares paid by transit and suburban rail passengers cover less than 70 percent of total expenditure for urban public transportation systems by governments, railroads, and transit companies, with the difference consisting of public subsidies in many of the larger metropolitan areas and losses suffered by private rail and transit companies. With rising operating costs and large-scale subsidy of new investment in these systems, the prospect is for the deficits to rise appreciably relative to fare revenue in coming years.

---

3. The reader will recognize that congestion costs indicate a situation in which the marginal costs of resource use to the economy exceed the average costs confronting each user, a situation with substantial external diseconomies that calls for pricing on the basis of marginal costs, if resource allocation is to be efficient. Note that efficiency in resource allocation does not require elimination of all congestion, but requires only that users pay for the costs of congestion. It is likely that the costs of eliminating *all* congestion in urban transportation would exceed the costs, in delay and discomfort, imposed by congestion.

The real point is that peak-hour, CBD-oriented private auto use is heavily subsidized from gasoline taxes and other user charges collected from off-peak motorists and motorists who use other parts of the urban highway network, and this subsidy is far greater than that received by peak-hour users of public transportation. In effect, highway users in our third market —the one in which there is virtually no competition from public transportation—are taxed in order to help the private auto undercut public transportation in the competitive, peak-hour, CBD-oriented second market. A consumer decides on his method for making an individual trip on the basis of the costs, speed, and comfort of the alternatives for that trip, and the pricing systems we use encourage him to use his car far more often that would be the case with better pricing systems. Until quite recently, governments have responded to the apparent consumer preferences and have invested heavily in CBD-oriented freeways, while permitting public transportation systems to deteriorate.

This response has been facilitated by the institutional arrangements affecting access to capital for improving transportation services. Since the 1920s, the basic way of financing highway investment has been through the state governments, which impose gasoline and vehicle taxes on a statewide basis on all highway users and tap this pool to improve selected portions of a very large highway network. Since 1957, the federal government has used a similar system on a nationwide basis. In contrast, investment in public transportation systems (until the last few years) has had to be financed from the revenues of individual private transit and railroad companies or from the limited financial resources of central-city governments. They have not had access to nationwide, statewide, or even metropolitan-area-wide pools of funds.

The revival of interest in public transportation in the 1960s, almost without exception, has been accompanied by institu-

tional changes designed to improve access to investment funds
—federal aid to mass transportation under legislation adopted
in 1964; state government financing in the northeastern states;
metropolitan-area-wide financing in San Francisco, Washington, and other areas. Without such changes in access to capital,
it is difficult to believe that major improvements in public
transportation services could be made. Without such improvements, speed, comfort, and accessibility of public transportation would continue to deteriorate relative to the alternative
presented by the private auto.

Urban Transportation and Urban Development

Even if the alternative modes of urban transportation did
compete on even terms, some people would argue that investment in urban transportation systems should not be guided by
apparent preferences of users, that is, should not be guided by
a "market solution." They argue that transportation creates
major external costs and benefits, in addition to the costs and
benefits realized by individual users themselves. There are
obvious external costs, like the effects on air pollution, but the
externalities most important to this argument concern the form
of development in urban areas. The claim is that different
forms of transportation have different (and quantitatively
large) effects on how an urban area develops. Therefore,
urban transportation systems must be planned to help foster
specified land-use and population-distribution objectives.
Transportation decisions can no more be left to the market
than can other urban planning decisions, such as the location
of parks or zoning.

The opposite view holds that most benefits and costs of
urban transportation are really internal to users and that therefore the appropriate policy is to follow the evident preferences

of present and prospective users (typically preferences at low or zero prices; but that is another matter).[4] Transportation is seen as population and activity serving, rather than as developmental. At least this is so for the characteristic large American urban area, where it is possible to get from any one point to any other point with considerable facility, and the issue is really one of rather marginal changes in relative accessibility within an urban area. This is obviously not the case in a newly developing region or in an underdeveloped country with a primitive transportation system.

It should be clear that neither extreme position is wholly valid. What in fact is the connection between changing transportation technology and the changing form of urban areas? As pointed out in Chapter 2, in the early history of American cities, the effect of transportation technology was quite evident. In the earliest years, most of the larger cities were located at harbors, portages, or heads of navigation—places where goods and people had to shift from one form of water transportation to overland transportation or to another form of water transportation. And, by and large, cities did stay close to the water as they grew, because of the ease of movement that these locations provided.

The advent of the streetcar and urban and suburban rail transportation permitted very rapid extensions of the area of urban development; it allowed urban development to move in different directions, away from water and beyond the distance

---

4. An efficient "market solution" of this type does not rule out subsidy. In the absence of congestion, urban transportation systems would be subject to increasing returns. That is, marginal cost would be below average cost. Optimal pricing is based on marginal cost, and in this situation, optimal pricing would require subsidies to encourage more use of underutilized facilities. The absence of congestion is, of course, not the usual case; with congestion, the optimal price is above average cost, not below it, with profit rather than subsidies the result.

that could be covered on foot. The whole level of accessibility was raised to a new plane. The suburban railroads permitted settlement to take place much further out than had been the case previously, with communities of commuters strung out along the main rail lines; the communities tended to remain small, because the means of transportation was inherently an expensive one. The advent of the automobile opened things up still more, because urban development could grow away from the fixed lines of rail transportation and away from water communications.

Each of these was a wholly new form of transportation technology, and their widespread availability led to major changes in the form of urban development. But now that ownership of motor vehicles is widespread, and very extensive road and transit networks actually exist, how much can transportation changes shape the form of urban areas in the foreseeable future? There is agreement that transportation did shape urban development markedly in the past; there is no such agreement as to whether it continues to do so.[5]

Skeptics take the position that the decentralizing forces at work in urban areas currently are so powerful that transportation cannot do more than serve these forces. The lesser importance of the CBD leads to less demand for public transportation

---

5. The argument is reminiscent of Edward Gibbon's observation on the date at which divine intervention into human affairs ended:

  . . . since every friend to revelation is persuaded of the reality, and every reasonable man is convinced of the cessation, of miraculous powers, it is evident that there must have been *some period* in which they were either suddenly or gradually withdrawn from the Christian church. . . . The conversion of Constantine is the era which is most usually fixed by Protestants. The more rational divines are unwilling to admit the miracles of the fourth, whilst the more credulous are unwilling to reject those of the fifth century.

  The Portable Gibbon: The Decline and Fall of the Roman Empire (New York: Viking, 1955), pp. 282–283.

and more demand for automobile transportation. Public policies that emphasize highway building reflect demand, rather than shape the urban environment. It is argued that the decentralizing forces are so strong that improved public transportation can have no perceptible effect on the pattern of urban development.[6]

The forces making for decentralization were noted in Chapter 2: the change in manufacturing technology in the direction of spread out, low-density, single-level plants; the desire on the part of ordinary people for more spacious living, and the prevalence of the higher incomes necessary to support more spacious living; and the fact that once people do start to move out in large numbers, other jobs and economic activity that serve this population will follow the population out. It is claimed that had less money been invested in highway transportation in recent years and more in public transportation and rail facilities, the trends toward decentralization would not have changed appreciably. This implies that had any given urban area adopted the policy of investing less in highways and more in other forms of transportation, some economic activity—notably manufacturing—probably would have shifted to different urban areas, to smaller places where the existing highway network would support highway-oriented manufacturing activities in single-level plants.

The argument has much merit. It is supported by the observation that a significant amount of new investment in manufacturing plants in the outer parts of urban areas is not along the lines of new freeways but along *existing,* rather second-rate, highway transportation facilities. Similarly, this is true of much suburban residential development: if transportation is

6. For a comprehensive statement of this argument, see J. R. Meyer, J. F. Kain, and M. Wohl, *The Urban Transportation Problem* (Cambridge, Mass.: Harvard University Press, 1965), part I.

responsible, then it is highway investment in the 1920s and 1930s that accounts for housing in the 1960s.

However, there are at least two reasons for hesitation in wholly accepting the proposition that transportation has little effect on urban form. First, individual location decisions by both businesses and individuals are made in response to the transportation services actually offered. During the last twenty years, there have been tremendous improvements in highway service, but very little, if any, improvement in public transportation service. For the great majority of trips of all kinds in nearly all urban areas, not excluding trips in peak hours to CBDs, travel by automobile is substantially faster than travel by the alternative modes, whether bus, subway, or suburban rail. Auto travel is almost always more comfortable and has an immense competitive edge in its flexibility of scheduling and door-to-door delivery capability.

Thus, it is not surprising that there has been as much decentralization in metropolitan areas with extensive public transportation systems, like Chicago, as in those without much public transportation service, like Los Angeles, in the past twenty years. The public transportation service is a decidedly inferior good, one that people will reject as soon as they can afford to. But what if there were drastic improvements in the *quality* of public transportation services?

This is not unlikely, at least in some urban areas. For example, in the New York area during the next decade, suburban rail speeds (on some lines) will be greatly increased, so much so that typical trips will take about one-half the door-to-door time they now require. This will make it much more attractive to live near the suburban rail line, rather than at a considerable distance from the line (because the travel between home and station will not get any faster), and no doubt some people will choose higher-density living in the villages in preference to lower-density living further from the railroad.

Also, because it will be more attractive to live in the sector of the metropolitan area having the high-speed service, that sector will tend to have higher-density development.

Improvement in the quality of transportation will not necessarily bolster the position of the central city as a residential location. It is much easier to increase greatly the speed of suburban rail service than it is to do the same for any other form of public transportation. The future may see an enhancement of the comparative advantage of locations close to the high-speed suburban rail service vis-à-vis outlying areas not near rail service and those parts of the central city at some distance from the CBD served only by conventional public transportation. In the largest central cities even now, it takes longer to reach the CBD from the outer parts of the central city than it does from the suburban areas served by the suburban rail lines or buses operated on freeways. The prospect is that great improvements in suburban rail speeds will considerably worsen the competitive position of these outer parts of the central city. But this, too, represents an impact of transportation changes on the form of urban development.

A second reason for questioning the evidence that shows transportation to have had little impact on urban form in recent years relates to pricing of transportation services. Individuals making residential location decisions surely do consider, as one of the costs of housing, the costs of traveling to work. If the costs actually paid by motorists for peak-hour use of CBD-oriented freeways located far out at the edge of the metropolitan area are very low, then distant housing subdivisions are likely to be relatively more attractive than otherwise. If the costs paid by motorists are low compared to the fares paid by rail commuters, subdivisions located far from the fixed rail lines are likely to be relatively more attractive than otherwise.

It is difficult to deny that very large changes in the structure of prices confronting users of transportation services would have some effect on location decisions. But it would be equally difficult to advocate such major changes in transportation prices if the existing price structure reflected the full resource costs of the different modes of transportation reasonably adequately. However, such is not the case, as the preceding section of this chapter shows. An economically efficient transportation pricing system—one in which all modes confront users with the full resource costs of their decisions—would involve very large increases in the cost of peak-hour, CBD-oriented auto commuting.

Thus, the highly dispersed form of residential development characteristic of most American urban areas, involving heavy auto use even for commuting to work, is not necessarily independent of changeable transportation characteristics. Auto use is faster, more comfortable, and relatively cheaper than the present alternatives and is consistent with one pattern of urban development. If auto use were no longer faster, more comfortable, and cheaper, it is a fair bet that some consumers would choose other transport modes, and some of these would alter their residential location choices as well. No doubt many would prefer very low densities even so, but the urban fabric is the sum total of many individual choices. If significant numbers of people opt for the higher densities made more attractive by improvements in public transportation and changes in pricing, the urban fabric will look quite different twenty or thirty years hence than it would otherwise.

The Revival of Mass Transportation

From the outset of World War II until the early 1960s, investment in public transportation was pretty much a holding operation: new buses and rail cars were bought to replace aging existing fleets, and rail lines were rehabilitated to make up for maintenance neglected during the 1940s. The picture has changed rather abruptly recently, and there is once again substantial new (not merely replacement) investment in public transportation. The investment is taking various forms: rapid transit extensions and other major improvements in those cities now having rapid transit systems; substantial investment in improvements in suburban rail service in New York, Philadelphia, and Chicago; and development of wholly new rapid transit systems in cities that have not had them (like San Francisco and Washington) at costs that are enormously high relative to the number of riders they will serve.

These high costs reflect the fact that the market is indeed a limited one, confined to peak-hour, CBD-oriented service. The limited nature of the market explains the difficulty in mustering public support for massive expansion of public transportation until recently; after all, in a large metropolitan area, only a small fraction of the adult population will use the new systems regularly. Thus, voters have been understandably slow to accept investments that require large-scale public subsidy.

This subsidization is a new thing to a considerable extent, although not entirely. The older rapid transit lines in New York, Boston, and Philadelphia were constructed with a fair amount of public subsidy to begin with, although some of the subsidy was disguised and indirect. But suburban rail lines were not subsidized, nor were transit facilities in most other places. And outside New York and Boston, transit systems were expected to cover operating expenses and a fair proportion of debt-service costs as well. The new picture involves subsidy for suburban rail operating expenses as well as major capital improvements; subsidy for construction of wholly new systems; and a reasonable prospect that some of these new systems may require operating subsidies as well.

What explains the revival of interest in forms of urban transportation requiring large-scale public subsidy? It must be noted that the willingness to subsidize public transportation is not confined to the big-city governments in whose constituencies the main beneficiaries—the users—are important and articulate groups. State governments are providing direct and indirect subsidies, notably in the northeastern states and in California. And significant amounts of federal government subsidy are provided under legislation enacted in the 1960s. This is striking, for it suggests that Congress perceives a national interest in dealing with problems that are really important only in a small number of very large cities.

There seem to be two explanations for the revival. One is the strong conviction that there are very substantial external benefits created by improving transportation to the CBDs, such as the creation of jobs and protection of tax bases. If it is important to increase the capacity of transportation facilities to the CBD, to increase travel speeds and to make travel less uncomfortable, this conceivably might be done by greatly expanding CBD-oriented freeway capacity. But the choice now is increasingly for expanded and improved public transportation. The common statement is that this is because (1) it would be impossible to handle the traffic volumes contemplated solely by building more highways, and (2) investment in public transportation facilities would be much cheaper per passenger. To economists, the former statement is not an acceptable one: when popular writers and public officials use the term "impossible" to describe a public policy alternative, they usually mean that in their estimation a physically possible action has ridiculously high political and economic costs.

The costs of a highway solution can be high indeed, if both the direct money costs of highway building and the indirect social costs are considered. The latter include the displacement of residents and businesses, the destruction of old neighborhoods with their web of established social relationships, and the ugliness of huge highway structures. For the largest metropolitan areas, a pure highway solution to the CBD transportation problem typically involves substantial construction work and land acquisition in and around the CBD itself, extensive disruption of established moderate-income neighborhoods in the central city, and massive construction through the older, close-in, but high-income, suburbs.

It is not necessarily true that, in all cases, the highway solution would be the more expensive one, even if all costs are considered. What is true is that our institutional arrangements do not provide for anything like adequate compensation for those who would suffer from massive expansion of CBD-oriented highway facilities. It is not enough to pay for real property in the way of a freeway at market prices and to make payments to occupants for moving expenses. Truly adequate compensation would be far more expensive, for it would permit displaced people, businesses, and institutions to recreate their old environments in a new (and equally desirable) location. Low-income people would be protected from the need to pay more for housing; businesses would be compensated for loss of custom; there would be compensation for loss of visual amenity and neighborhood relationships. In the absence of full compensation for losses, the losers hotly resist the highway solution. The result is that this solution then becomes politically "impossible."

In this light, the public transportation solution, despite the heavy subsidy, appears highly attractive. Moreover, it is usually combined with the argument that heavy investment in public transportation will divert some of the present auto traffic and thus relieve congestion for the remaining traffic, which will then be able to flow more rapidly.

The second explanation for the willingness to provide large subsidies for a public transportation solution might be called the "parallel subsidy" argument. That is, legislators, public officials, and pro-highway interest groups recognize that there are the biases in existing public policy discussed in this chapter (although they hardly publicly proclaim this recognition). They are unwilling to alter the arrangements surrounding the planning and financing of highways, but instead offer some degree of parallel subsidy to public transportation.

Whether this is a sensible public policy solution depends upon the extent and nature of externalities, the controversy discussed in the previous section. If the external benefits, above and beyond the benefits realized by users, are minor, then it is clear that the preferred solution would be a policy of no subsidy all-round. If this were the case, parallel subsidy would produce a level of investment in urban transportation greater than could be justified by the benefits to both users and the public at large, a prime example of inefficient allocation of real resources.

On the other hand, if the external benefits are substantial, there will be economic inefficiency if there is *not* subsidization. Ideally, the degree of subsidy to the modes of urban transportation should be proportional to the external benefits; if the external benefits from one form of transportation are small and those from another are large, the subsidy to the latter should be much the larger.

There is no agreement, as we have seen, about the nature and extent of the external benefits. However, there is some reason to suppose that external benefits from public transportation are relatively large and those from the auto alternative are relatively small,[7] in the competitive, peak-hour, CBD-

---

7. Indeed, the external benefits may be negative, and substantially so: increased air pollution, uncompensated disruption of neighborhoods, and so on.

oriented, urban transportation submarket. For one thing, improved public transportation can serve those without cars—
the very poor, the young, the old, the infirm; serving the help-
less is usually considered a positive social benefit. For another,
subsidy to public transportation may encourage less dispersed
patterns of urban development and thus economize on the use
of urban land, which should also be counted as a social benefit.
Then, too, subsidy to public transportation may do a better
job of fostering the redevelopment of established points of
concentration like CBDs, outlying business districts, and older
suburban villages. If such places have extensive public facilities, utility lines, and the like already in place and not in need
of replacement, redevelopment efforts can exploit these elements of sunk costs which (remember Chapter 1) involve zero
resource costs in the present and future.

All transportation subsidies, to any mode, tend to create
external benefits in the form of increases in the value of the
land better served by the subsidized transport. These benefits
are captured by those who own the land at the time the transportation service is improved. This seems to be generally
recognized by CBD property owners in large cities, who often
are vigorous supporters of subsidy to urban transportation.
Because public transportation subsidies are usually financed in
considerable part from local taxes on property and because
such taxes are typically disproportionately high on CBD property, there is some economic logic as well as equity in public
transportation subsidies, in this respect. In contrast, taxes on
land owners seldom finance any of the subsidy to peak-hour,
CBD-oriented motorists. Thus, if our financing mechanisms
are taken as given, the case for subsidizing public transportation is stronger than the case for subsidizing the automobile
alternative.

Directions for Public Policy

However this may be, continued heavy investment in both highways and public transportation is likely to occur in many large urban areas for the foreseeable future. The open options in urban transportation policy fall into two classes. First, what can be done to make the settled policy of parallel development of the two forms work better? Second, are there supplemental policies, not necessarily involving massive investment, that make sense?

No matter how great the extent of subsidy overall, there is a strong case for sensible pricing policies to encourage good utilization of both highway and public transportation facilities, new as well as existing ones. The need for this in the case of highways is clear from the earlier discussion: the existing pricing system, largely the gasoline tax, does nothing to help sort out those motorists who really have pressing needs to use the most congested streets and roads at the most crowded hours from those whose needs are far less pressing. We do in fact ration urban highway space now—those who cannot afford the delays or cannot stomach the crowding are rationed out, which means that priority goes to those who value their time least, and service is slow for everyone. One response to this, in addition to heavy investment in new facilities, consists of increasingly numerous calls for restriction of entry to central areas by law or regulation, barring private cars except for specified classes of owners.[8]

In general in our society, we ration by price rather than by regulation or congestion: he who values the use of the resource

---

8. By March 1969, even the U.S. secretary of transportation, whose occupational bias is strongly *against* restrictions on transport users, was warning that restriction on highway entry into CBDs of large cities was likely to be necessary.

most highly bids it away from others who prefer to use their incomes for other purposes. Rationing by price has some major advantages, for it is impersonal and administratively simple, as well as efficient in an economic sense. In contrast, administration of legal controls on entry would require large numbers of hairsplitting decisions by a public body that would have to distinguish between high- and low-priority users. There does not seem to be any clear reason to avoid rationing by price in this case, other than inertia and the absence of good pricing mechanisms.

A number of such pricing mechanisms have been proposed. They include highly sophisticated electronic sensing devices mounted on cars and in the streets, which would result in computer-written monthly bills to motorists (or other price signals), charging them more for the use of congested routes in crowded hours. A fair amount of research on this has been done in Britain and the United States, and the systems appear technically feasible; the British government and the Greater London Council have been considering their use in central London. Less far-out proposals include high toll charges at peak hours on main access routes, which is especially feasible where there are bridges and tunnels on the access routes (as in New York), and heavy taxes on parking facilities in central areas (because motorists do not drive to the CBD simply to cruise around, but to park there).

Indeed, more rational pricing of parking in congested areas, both within and outside the CBD, makes a great deal of sense. In general, American cities encourage and subsidize parking at the worst times and places: they permit on-street parking free or at nominal meter charges; they subsidize public off-street facilities; they require private developers to include off-street parking facilities that will be used mainly at the most congested times of day; and they undertax land used for parking lots. They thus provide a positive incentive for travel by private car in the presence of congested conditions. It would not be difficult to devise policies that did precisely the reverse, while still making available ample parking space at less congested times, such as on Saturdays and weekday evenings.

More sensible transit pricing is also both possible and desirable. The flat transit fare characteristic of American cities ignores the fact that the costs of providing the service vary with the time of day, direction of travel, and length of trip. As noted earlier, many of the off-peak trips impose virtually no cost on transit system operators: the crews and vehicles are in service and are paid for whether the buses and trains are two-thirds full or two-thirds empty. It is a universal experience that when the flat transit fares are increased, patronage in off-peak hours falls off appreciably, while patronage in peak hours and directions changes little. This means that riders are being driven away by higher prices (fares) despite the fact that their use entails little or no resource costs—an appalling example of a "money illusion" at work.

This could easily be overcome by fare differentials based on time, direction, and distance. Modern technology makes possible electronic fare-collection systems that can handle such differentials. There is a special reason for considering such pricing mechanisms now. The heavy investment in public transportation systems now underway or planned is designed to handle peak-hour travel. It will produce vast capacity for low-cost accommodation of off-peak riders, and this capacity will go largely unutilized under the flat-fare system. To be sure, the demand for off-peak service is limited, but low off-peak fares could help to tap even this limited market.

It is frequently asserted that differential transit fares would hurt the poor who must use the transit system and must use it at peak hours. In general, this assertion is invalid. First, the poor tend to live closer to the center and make shorter trips; a distance differential would tend to help, rather than hurt, the poor. Second, many of the poorest people travel in the off-peak hours or travel against the main flow of traffic. Some of them are not employed at all; others work nonstandard hours, like cleaning women in office buildings; and still others work outside the CBD. Third, the poor tend to be more dependent on the transit system for nonwork trips, most of which would be cheaper than they now are with a differential fare arrangement.

There is also a more general answer to the assertion. While it is good public policy to avoid harshly burdening low-income families, it is difficult and inefficient to require that *every* one of our social institutions deliberately favor the poor, however small the money effect is. The way to help low-income families is to improve their employment prospects and directly ensure them a minimum income level (see Chapter 3), not to try to manipulate all policies and institutions to this end.

A call for economic pricing of public transportation services appears in direct contradiction to widespread public sentiment about transit fares in the early 1970s. As noted earlier public transportation deficits are substantial in a number of large cities, and they appear to be getting worse. Transit operating costs are mainly labor costs, so the general rapid rise in wages and fringe benefits in recent years has had a sharp impact on transit costs. Moreover, there are few remaining opportunities to increase productivity to offset rising labor costs, as was done by the elimination of streetcars with two-man crews, which was widely done in the 1950s and early 1960s. Awareness of rising costs and the adverse effects of fare increases on transit use has led to much greater public acceptance of the case for operating, as well as capital, subsidies to transit. The extreme version of this is the argument for "free transit"—that is, zero fares—increasingly heard in cities in North America and Western Europe.

The arguments for "free transit" include the external benefits argument discussed above: high transit use promotes economic activity in the CBD and keeps property values high, thus justifying heavy subsidy from taxes levied on CBD economic activity and real property. Also, high transit use is said to be necessary in order to minimize the air pollution generated by auto use in central parts of metropolitan areas. It is becoming clear that in many, if not most, large cities, achievement of acceptable air-quality standards may require restrictions on auto use within the next decade. Also, it is argued that transit fares are equivalent to highly regressive taxes that burden the poor more than would almost any conceivable form of taxation used to finance transit service. Finally, proponents have pointed out that fare-collection costs are very high (estimated by some to account for as much as one-fifth of labor costs in subway systems), and these amount to what economists call "dead-weight losses." That is, they are resource costs that produce no service or consumer satisfaction whatever.

But there are also persuasive arguments against "free transit." First, it is by no means clear that the external benefits not realized by the transit users themselves are all that great. For example, with zero fares, wage levels, profits, and land values in CBDs might all adjust by amounts no greater than the aggregate reduction in fares, leaving the community as a whole no better off. Also, the air pollution argument is not conclusive. One of the worst environmental problems facing the country today is the ecological damage done by increases in the amount of electric power generated in urban areas. The increased electric energy needed to provide motive power for the new and expanded subway systems that would be necessary if there were no auto traffic in central areas is by no means a trivial environmental concern. More generally, it is open to serious question whether "free transit" in fact would attract enough additional transit use to produce the external benefits, even if those benefits are real. There is strong evidence that the demand for CBD-oriented, journey-to-work transit service is rather price-inelastic, at least in the price range implied by proposals to reduce fares by 50 cents or less. One study of Chicago auto commuters suggested that even zero fares would divert only a small fraction of drivers from cars to transit.[9] This is not surprising, because speed and flexibility are likely to be the most important costs and benefits considered by users.

Second, there are dead-weight losses involved in the taxes that might be levied to substitute for the revenue from transit fares. Virtually all taxes distort economic decision making to some extent and therefore should not be recommended lightly as superior on efficiency grounds to prices paid by users that are inefficient because they have high collection costs. And the taxes required to finance "free transit" in cities with well-developed transit systems would be high indeed. In New York, replacement of fares (even after allowance for savings in fare-collection costs) would require the city to double its 3-percent sales tax or its taxes on business and personal income or increase its property taxes by one-fourth.

Finally, "free transit" is economically inefficient in a most basic way: it is an effort to encourage people to use more transportation services, and the resources required to provide such services, regardless of the purpose, direction, or cost of the trip. It is hard to see what public purpose there is in stimu-

9. Leon N. Moses and Harold F. Williamson, Jr., "Value of Time, Choice of Mode and the Subsidy Issue in Urban Transportation," *Journal of Political Economy* 71 (1963): 247–264.

lating more urban travel, for transportation is not an end product, one of the good things in life. It is rather a means to other ends and, as such, should be economized on, like the use of electricity, water, computers, pencils, and all the many other goods and services that are not enjoyed for their own sake. Economic pricing can result in such economizing, and selective subsidies can elicit the external benefits that are real and important. "Free transit," in contrast, must lead us away from Pareto-efficiency.

Nonprice Policy Options

In addition to reforms in transportation pricing, there are other ways in which the established policy of heavy investment in both highways and public transportation can be made to work better. These consist largely of technological improvement. For example, positive control of entry onto freeways, activated by electronic sensing and control devices, could keep them free flowing, even in the most congested hours. It is far more efficient to make each motorist wait ten or fifteen minutes for freeway entry (and thereby encourage some motorists to find alternative routes that are less congested), than to permit the clogging and drastic reduction in average speeds, often to less than ten miles an hour, that are now characteristic of freeways in rush hours in the largest cities.

If there is to be heavy investment in public transportation, there is every reason to consider radically new types of public transportation potentially capable of much higher speeds and other standards, rather than simply to invest in a transit technology substantially unchanged since the 1920s, as is now being done. Research done in connection with the federal government's program to improve ground transportation in the Northeast corridor—between Boston and Washington—

suggests possible intraurban applications of advanced technology. For example, the gravity-vacuum tube system now being tested would permit average trip speeds as high as ninety miles an hour, with frequent and relatively closely spaced stops; the system would utilize deep tunnels (and thus involve almost no disruption to established structures and facilities) and have high passenger capacity and low power requirements.[10]

A variety of supplemental policies, not requiring massive investment in new facilities, are available, especially to improve urban transportation services to the poor.[11] One of the simplest is to provide relatively modest subsidies to reorient bus services so that they better serve the poor by providing better and faster connections between ghetto areas and outlying job locations and by increasing the frequency of service to non-CBD destinations. It has been observed that "the major difficulty facing the poor and particularly the ghetto poor is not that transit is too expensive, but that it is all too frequently unavailable in forms or services required."[12] This is because most bus lines converge on the CBD, as the old streetcar lines did years ago. For ghetto residents not traveling to the CBD, this means slow travel along indirect routing, with transfers required.

Since many low-income people do not work in the CBD even now, and since job opportunities are expanding in the suburbs, it is obvious that private automobile transportation

---

10. Lawrence K. Edwards, "High Speed Tube Transportation," *Scientific American*, August 1965, pp. 30–40.
11. A good summary review can be found in John F. Kain and John R. Meyer, "Interrelationships of Transportation and Poverty: Summary of Conference on Transportation and Poverty," Harvard University Program on Regional and Urban Economics, Discussion Paper no. 39, November 1968.
12. Kain and Meyer, "Interrelationships," p. 18.

does have and can have a large role in solving the transportation problems of the central-city poor. It is not inconceivable that subsidizing auto ownership for poorer urban groups might be the most economical solution to the immediate problems. This could be done in a number of ways, for example, by lowering the cost of credit to low-income car purchasers so they can buy newer cars (cheap old cars are seldom truly low-annual-cost cars).[13] Or cars might be rented or leased on a subsidized basis. Since auto insurance rates tend to be very high in inner-city areas where the poor are concentrated, auto insurance reforms designed to reduce premiums—which reforms are worthwhile in their own right—could also contribute to this end.

Modernized jitney cab services, with or without subsidy, could also help the poor. Indeed, the whole area of taxicab and jitney service is one with considerable possibilities. Nearly all American cities (except for Washington, D.C.) severely restrict taxi service in various ways, but most notably in limiting the number of cabs. Whatever the original reasons, the results coincide with what economic theory would have predicted: fares are high, use is confined to people with relatively high incomes, and the owners of the franchises have high monopoly profits.[14]

If there were no restriction on the provision of taxi and jitney service (other than such basic things as requirements for adequate insurance coverage and driver licensing), several types of benefits might result. First, there would surely be

---

13. Lowering the cost of credit to low-income people is, of course, the most popular form of subsidy in the housing field.
14. The extent of the monopoly profits and the losses in economic efficiency have been estimated in quantitative terms for one such city—Chicago. See Edmund W. Kitch, Marc Isaacson, and Daniel Kasper, "The Regulation of Taxicabs in Chicago," *Journal of Law and Economics* 14 (October 1971): 285–350.

much more service. In some Latin American cities, jitneys are a major part of the transportation system: in Caracas, Venezuela, for example, they provide nearly 20 percent of the total service, as compared to the 2-3 percent (or less) provided by taxis in most American cities. The poor, not the rich, are the usual users of jitney service. Second, the expanded service would offer a considerable number of jobs to low-income workers and could significantly reduce the unemployment rate in some cities. Third, if many taxi drivers owned their cabs and operated them on a part-time basis (as a second job), and if the off-duty cab could double as a family car —both of these conditions hold in Washington—incomes are raised, costs of auto ownership are lowered, and the mobility of residents of low-income neighborhoods is increased.

This is surely no panacea. It is, instead, an illustration of some of the economic considerations suggested in Chapter 1: the advantages of relatively simple solutions to problems, solutions that have near-term rather than remote payoffs, maximize the use of existing capital, can be easily reversed if they prove failures, can be applied incrementally rather than all at once on a massive scale, and do not preclude future changes in technology, preferences, or living patterns.

PART III

RAISING THE MONEY

8

Financing Urban Government

The policies for the resolution of urban problems discussed in this book are, for the most part, *governmental* policies. That is, they require action by some governmental entity. In some cases, the governmental action required is no more than alteration of the rules governing private decision making, like zoning or building codes. But in most cases, the need is for governments to use resources for common purposes, by investing in facilities, providing day-to-day services, making income transfers to needy people, and paying subsidies to achieve specified purposes.

The concern of this chapter is with the means of financing governmental use of resources in urban areas. How can and should governments assemble these resources? What are the mechanisms that should be used to transfer funds to the public sector from the private individuals and businesses possessing income and wealth? The financing of government activities is among the most dismal aspects of economics as the "dismal science," for the solutions are bound to make many unhappy with the outcome. Most people would prefer that others pay the costs of public services, however desirable the services may

223

be. No doubt people have similar preferences for not paying for private goods and services, but ordinarily they have no choice: either they pay the price established in the market, or they do without. No such self-evident limitation exists with regard to public services. The political process separately determines who benefits from public services and who pays for them. It is only in rare cases that the beneficiaries from, and payers for, a particular service are identical.

There can therefore be no ideal solution to the problem of financing government. However, it is possible to use economic reasoning to suggest solutions that are clearly superior to ones that now exist. Previous chapters have suggested that there are two serious types of deficiencies in existing arrangements. One relates to the governmental machinery used to provide and raise money for urban public services, more specifically, the over-heavy reliance on local governments with limited geographic scope. Another relates to the specific financing devices employed by local governments; the worst problems are presented by the most important such device, the property tax.

The Urban Public Sector

The difficulties can best be understood by examining what it is that governments spend money for now, which levels of government do the spending, and how this spending is financed. In the following paragraphs, the discussion will deal with the whole range of civilian public expenditure in the United States, not just that in urban areas. However, ours is an urban society and well over 75 percent of all civilian public expenditure either occurs in urban areas or is made in behalf of urban-area residents (for example, at state mental hospitals, often located in rural surroundings, but serving the largely urban population of a state).

In 1970–71, American governments spent a total of $250 billion for civilian purposes, that is, excluding defense, international, space, veterans, and related activities (see Table 8-1). Roughly one-third of this spending was done by the

TABLE 8-1 *Civilian Public Expenditure in the United States, 1970-1971 (In Billions of Dollars)*

	Federal Government Expenditure[a]	State-Local Governments	
		Expenditure	Federal Aid
All Civilian Programs[b]	83.7	166.6	27.5
Economic-Stabilization Activities[c]	5.3	5.7	0.7
Income-Redistribution Activities:	50.0	32.9	12.2
Health and Welfare	3.1[d]	29.4	10.6
Social Security, etc.[e]	44.9	0.9	—
Housing Programs	1.9	2.6	1.6
Public Schools	—	41.8	4.2
Resource-Allocation Activities:	28.4	86.3	10.4
Highways	0.3	18.1	5.0
Natural Resources	5.4	3.1	0.6
Higher Education	—	14.8	2.6
Postal Service	8.7	—	—
Police, Correction, and Fire	0.6	9.4	0.2
Transportation (except highways)	3.8	3.7	0.1
Water Supply and Water Treatment	—[f]	6.1	0.5
All Other	9.6	31.1	1.5

Note: Because of rounding, detail may not add to totals.

Source: Adapted from U.S. Census Bureau, *Governmental Finances in 1970-71* (1972).

[a]Direct expenditure only; grants to state-local governments spent by these units are shown in the last column.

[b]Excludes defense, international relations, space programs, veterans' services, interest on the federal debt (mainly war related), and employee retirement benefits.

[c]Includes farm price support and unemployment insurance activities.

[d]Excludes federal health research expenditure, assigned to "Resource Allocation."

[e]Includes state workmen's compensation and temporary disability programs, in addition to old-age, survivors, disability, and health insurance.

[f]Federal water programs included under "Natural Resources."

federal government and the rest by state and local governments. Forty years ago, the federal government accounted for only one-sixth of a much smaller total. The state government role has also expanded, although not as much as the federal role. But even so, local governments today are responsible for 40 percent of civilian public expenditure.

In Table 8-1, government civilian activities are classified on a basis that is now conventional among economists.[1] Governments are conceived as having three distinct overall objectives in the use of taxes and expenditures: to reduce fluctuations in economic activity; to change the distribution of income among individuals in the society from that produced by the workings of the private sector (because economic forces tend to produce a greater degree of inequality than the society is prepared to tolerate); and to change the allocation of resources so as to produce more of certain types of services and goods than would be supplied on a wholly private basis. In Table 8-1, expenditure for the public schools is shown as a fourth major class, not because the objectives are different, but because elementary and secondary education blends two objectives: providing more education for the populace in general and providing more education for children from lower-income families than their parents could possibly afford—an income-redistribution objective.

During prosperous periods, expenditure for economic stabilization activities, like unemployment insurance benefits, is understandably small; indeed pursuit of the economic stabilization objective is likely to involve raising federal taxes while *reducing* expenditure (as occured in 1968) in order to reduce inflationary pressures. In any event, this objective is

---

1. This approach was first developed by Richard A. Musgrave in *The Theory of Public Finance* (New York: McGraw-Hill, 1959), Chap. 1.

necessarily the province of the federal government, for state and local governments simply do not have the economic and financial powers necessary to buck economic trends.

The federal government's major civilian role (at least in 1970–1971) is in connection with income-redistribution activities. These are activities in which income is redistributed in two forms: direct money payments to the indigent, the aged, and the infirm; and the provision of health, welfare, and housing services, at little or no cost, to sectors of the population with incomes too low to secure such services at market prices.[2] The federal government is responsible for directly providing the bulk of the income-redistribution activities, in dollar terms. In addition, it finances more than one-third of the state-local sector's income-redistribution expenditure. Nevertheless, state and local governments spend very substantial amounts that they raise themselves for income-redistribution activities, especially when the income-redistribution aspect of the public schools is taken into account.

However, state-local expenditure is dominated by resource-allocation activities. The state and local governments overshadow the federal government in this respect; federal aid for resource-allocation activities is relatively minor. The federal government spends a lot for natural resource activities; it operates the postal service; it provides some air and water transportation facilities; it heavily aids highways and provides sizable amounts for higher education. But that list virtually exhausts its civilian-resource-allocation role. All the other resource-allocation activities, ranging from the public schools to garbage collection, are performed mainly by state and local

---

2. Many state and local health services are in theory open to the entire population. In practice, those who use the services without paying their full cost are heavily concentrated in the low-income population.

governments and are financed almost entirely from funds they themselves raise.

The distinction between the state governments and the local governments is an important one. This is illustrated in Table 8-2, which covers the income-redistribution activities, the pub-

TABLE 8-2   *Financing of Selected Urban Services, 1970-1971*

Selected Urban Services	Amounts Spent by Governments Actually Providing the Services (in billions)			How State-Local Spending Is Financed[a]		
	State	Local	State and Local	Federal Funds	State Funds	Local Funds
Income-Redistribution Activities:						
Welfare	$10.5	$ 7.7	$12.2	54%	35%	11%
Health and Hospitals	5.4	5.8	11.2	7	47	46
Housing Programs	—[b]	2.5	2.6	63	5	32
Public Schools	0.5	41.3	41.8	10	39	51
Resource-Allocation Activities:						
Police, Correction, and Fire	2.0	7.4	9.4	2	22	76
Transportation (except Highways)	0.3	3.4	3.7	5	11	84
Water Supply and Water Treatment	—[c]	6.1	6.1	8	2	90
Local Parks and Recreation	—[c]	2.1	2.1	2	5	93
Sanitation (except Sewerage)	—	1.4	1.4	—	—	100
Libraries	0.1	0.7	0.8	10	13	77
TOTALS	$18.8	$78.5	$97.3	18%	32%	50%

Note: Because of rounding, detail may not add to totals.
Source: Adapted from U.S. Census Bureau releases.
[a]These columns describe the source of funds for the state-local direct expenditure shown in the preceding columns. The federal government also makes the direct expenditure for federal programs shown in column 1, Table 8-1, for example, for the air-traffic-control system. The federal funds shown in this table include only federal aid to state and local government.
[b]Less than $50 million.
[c]There is some direct state-government expenditure for urban water supply and for urban parks, but it is small and difficult to separate out from published data.

lic schools, and those resource-allocation activities that are heavily concentrated in urban areas (the principal exclusions are highways and higher education, both primarily the responsibility of state governments). The heavy responsibilities of the local governments are striking: they directly provide the bulk of public services in urban areas, and the state government role is a very modest one aside from the income-redistribution activities. If one is concerned with the scope and quality of public services in urban America (highways and higher education aside), one must look to the local governments.

To be sure, the local governments are aided by grants from both federal and state governments. They end up financing, from their own resources, only about one-fourth of the income-redistribution activities of state-local governments combined. Nearly one-half of local school costs are financed by the higher levels of government. But nearly all of the urban resource-allocation services are financed from local resources. In all, a formidable job of fund raising is left to American urban local governments. From local taxes, or from charges imposed for the services they provide, or by borrowing, they now (1973) raise roughly $500 per capita of the urban population.

Restructuring the Public Sector

What is wrong with this system of heavy local responsibility? If the system is to be changed, its defects must be serious ones, not trivial ones, for local self-government is a deeply seated tradition in the English-speaking world in general and in the United States in particular. And power to make decisions on taxes and public spending has always been the essential ingredient of self-government, from the revolutionary beginnings of this Republic and for centuries before that in English constitutional history. Moreover, in this era of concern for the individual and community vis-à-vis the large anonymous organizations—government and corporate—our tradition of heavy reliance on the most local of governments should not be discarded lightly.

However, this tradition has three major drawbacks in the contemporary world. First, it cannot adequately cope with "spillovers," or costs and benefits external to individual local government units. The benefits from many types of public services assigned to local governments spill over the boundaries of the governmental units providing the services. Equally important, the costs of dealing, by government action, with many social problems spill over the boundaries of the local governmental units that ostensibly are responsible for the resolution of the problem.

Second, there are tremendous disparities in taxable resources and expenditure requirements among the fifty states and, even more, among the 78,000 local government units in the United States. These lead to gross disparities in the levels of public services provided, even within a single metropolitan area; to gross disparities in tax rates that can influence the location of economic activity in undesirable ways; and to efforts (for example, by zoning for fiscal ends) to protect a relatively advantageous fiscal position by beggaring one's neighbors.

Third, the distribution of responsibility for providing public services among the three levels of government—federal, state, and local—does not correspond at all well with their respective tax-raising capabilities. Ours is an open economy in which people, businesses, and capital can freely move among its geographic sections. In such an economy, it is difficult at best for small governmental units to tax economic flows or activities that cross municipal and state lines. Moreover, very large differentials in tax levels within a single open economy cannot persist, because people and businesses will "vote with their feet" against such taxes, by moving to other places. The broader the geographic scope of a government, the less serious this problem is. For the federal government, the problem does not exist, and thus the federal government is free to impose very high tax rates indeed, such as individual income tax rates of 70 percent, taxes on corporate profits exceeding 40 percent, and payroll taxes exceeding 10 percent.

If, instead, lower levels of government tried to impose such levels of taxes, there would be very large differentials. For example, a metropolitan government in the Wilmington, Delaware, area could raise as much per capita as nearby Baltimore with income tax rates only half as high as in Baltimore. Who can doubt that many $15,000-a-year families, faced with tax differentials of $1,000 or more a year for identical levels of public services, would in fact "vote with their feet"?

The reality is that the federal government has great tax-raising capabilities, but only limited responsibilities for civilian public expenditure. At the other end of the spectrum, the local governments have severely circumscribed tax-raising capabilities to match their very heavy expenditure responsibilities. This situation has been called "fiscal imbalance."

Any restructuring of the public sector that shifts fiscal burdens to higher levels of government will alleviate all three types of defects of the present system: the inadequate handling of spillovers; disparities in service and tax levels; and fiscal imbalance among the levels of government. But the various defects call for somewhat different specific forms of restructuring.

SPILLOVERS

Almost all local public services provide *some* benefits to people who live outside a particular local government's boundaries, just as nearly all local taxes have *some* effects on outsiders. For some types of public services, however, the external benefits are very large relative to the internal ones. Where this is the case, it is not reasonable to expect that adequate levels of service will be provided. Voters in a community are unlikely to be willing to tax themselves heavily to provide services whose benefits are largely realized by others. If the decisions were made at a regional, state, or national level, voters in those larger areas might be entirely willing to do so, because the area in which the bulk of the benefits are realized and the area in which the taxes are collected would coincide. But when the decisions on services with heavy spillovers are made by small units of government, this is not the case. To economists, this is clearly inefficient decision making, which results in most cases in too little public expenditure.

There are two main classes of locally provided services with heavy spillovers. One is the range of services connected with human resource development: education, health and welfare services, and manpower training. Here the spillovers come from the fact that people do migrate, in large numbers, among areas, so that we all have an interest in seeing to it that ours is a healthy, well-educated population. Children raised in poverty with inadequate education and health care in one section of the country or one central city are highly likely to be living in other places in later years, bringing with them their poor health, low educational attainments, and generalized social problems.

The second class of services with heavy spillovers includes those in which the technology of the service itself makes it impossible to confine benefits and costs to small areas—services like environmental control, transportation, major parks and recreational facilities, and research and development activities. Public activities connected with air and water quality, for example, affect entire natural basins that have little to do with political boundary lines. Most governmental transportation services and facilities accommodate users from a variety of governmental jurisdictions. The benefits from medical research or the development of new technology for high-speed ground transportation similarly accrue over a wide area, perhaps the whole nation.

Education is by far the most expensive of the locally provided services affected with major spillovers. The great bulk of the benefits from public elementary and secondary schooling are realized outside the school district that provided the child's education. In fact, in the aggregate, Americans spend about 80 percent of their postschool years living in communities other than those in which they were educated. This would seem to suggest that 80 percent, not 50 percent (see Table 8-2), of the costs of the public schools should be met from federal and state—rather than local—funds. Because much of the movement of population is between states, the federal role should be a large one, perhaps 40 percent of the total, rather than 10 percent as at present.

On the other hand, a large fraction of the benefits from better schooling are internal to the child and his parents, not generalized *external* benefits to society. Thus, if parents recognize these benefits, they should be willing to pay the current costs of the schools from taxes levied each year, whether or not they or their children will be living in that particular school district in subsequent years. Ideally, therefore, the private benefits from education should be financed from local taxes, while the public or external benefits—in the form of the better-educated voting populace a democracy needs and the reduction in future poverty problems stemming from better education—should be financed from state or federal funds, especially the latter. The relative magnitude of private and public benefits is far from clear, however. It is a reasonable supposition that the public-to-private benefit ratio is quite high in poor regions and other areas (like large central cities) where poor children are concentrated, and quite low in affluent suburbs. This argues for a geographically differentiated system of school finance. Alternatively, it presents a case for the direct provision of federally financed education "vouchers" to the poor, under arrangements similar to the housing allowances discussed in Chapter 4.

The geographic spillovers from the directly income-redistributive services, particularly in health and welfare, have two geographic dimensions. One is the need for adequate levels of service for people in low income regions, in the rural South and Puerto Rico, for example—service levels that state and local governments in such relatively poor areas cannot afford by themselves. A second is newer—the concentration of low-income people in the large central cities of metropolitan areas in the North and West. This concentration results from migration from the poorer regions, the high birthrates among the urban minority-group poor and difficulty that these groups face in acquiring low-cost housing in suburban areas outside the large central cities. The fiscal burdens the central cities confront in providing health and welfare services are thus the result of cost "spillins"—they are providing for the poor on behalf of the whole nation or of whole metropolitan areas, in considerable part from their own fiscal resources.

This, of course, is not entirely new. In the nineteenth century, the large central cities were also great repositories of poor immigrants (from abroad). But then the central cities had a virtual monopoly on taxable economic activity in urban areas, in sharp contrast to the current situation. If taxes had to be imposed to serve the poor, the central city was the place that housed whatever wealth there was to tax; this is no longer true. Even more important, we are unwilling as a society to tolerate the extremes of poverty, poor health, and bad housing that characterized first-generation immigrants in the nineteenth and early twentieth centuries.

Overall, roughly 10 percent of the tax revenue of local governments is absorbed by their shares of the costs of redistributive services. And for the large central cities, this figure is closer to 25 percent. As a consequence, tax burdens in central cities tend to be higher than in suburbs, which affects their economic future and their ability to improve other public services, like education; in central cities, such services are typically now inferior to those in suburbs, unlike twenty years ago.[3] Even more important, these tax burden disparities tend to restrain improvements in health and welfare services. It is widely agreed that such services are grossly inadequate today. Yet no central city, however softhearted, can be softheaded enough to finance, from its own resources, the needed increases in the quantity, scope, and quality of income-redistribution activities, because to do so would widen the tax rate disparities.

Moreover, there are numerous cities, particularly the smaller ones with high concentrations of the poor (Newark, New Jersey, for example) that are simply too poor to finance from their own resources any increase in the level of such services, regardless of the tax rates imposed. Besides, when

---

3. Tax burdens in central cities are typically higher, relative to personal income, than in suburbs. The evidence is that, if the redistributive services were financed on an area-wide (or nationwide) basis, half of the tax burden disparity would be eliminated, on the average.

central cities tax their own residents to provide services to
the poor, they inevitably increase the tax burdens of the poor
themselves; this hardly makes sense.

The problems of the central cities, combined with the problem of the low-income regions, strongly suggest the need for
full federal financing of redistributive activities, rather than
the present system of heavy local responsibilities and even
heavier state government ones. In Chapter 3, the case for a
fully federalized system of income transfers was discussed; this
could be extended to apply equally well to compulsory federal
health insurance (not solely for the older part of the population) to supplant the present federal-state-local medical assistance programs. It is not feasible, of course, to expect the
federal government to directly provide *all* income-redistribution services. Remedial social services no doubt are best
carried out by local agencies, but even here, expanded federal
financing is essential.

The inadequacy of our present governmental machinery for
dealing with one type of "technological spillover" service—
those coping with the quality of the environment—was discussed in Chapter 6. Most services of this type are regional,
rather than nationwide, in the extent of benefit spillovers. For
example, air pollution is not a nationwide problem, but a
specific set of problems in each of a large number of natural
basins. The great bulk of the users of any segment of the
highway network travel within well-defined regions, rather
than over very long distances. The nature of the appropriate
public transportation system is defined by the characteristics
of the region in which the users live; a uniform nationwide
solution would make no sense at all.

The difficulty is that we have inadequate regional governmental machinery and therefore rely too heavily on relatively
small-area local governments. We also have instituted federal
programs to aid in solving problems that are essentially re-

gional, in part because it is politically easier to get federal aid than to restructure governmental machinery. Where the spillovers are interstate, as is often the case with water supply and water pollution, federal action is necessary. However, in many cases, the problems are confined to regions within states.

Ideally, the solution would be to develop the appropriate regional governmental agencies, interstate ones in some cases and intrastate ones, but covering whole metropolitan areas, in others. However, the success of efforts to develop metropolitan governmental arrangements in the United States has been very limited to date. Virtually the only general-purpose metropolitan governments that exist are in the South, and these have entailed little more than giving added responsibilities to county governments in a region where county government traditionally has been strong.

A substitute for regional government does exist—the state governments. Most of the states on the West Coast, around the Great Lakes, and in the Northeast are heavily urban. A state's boundaries may not coincide with natural service areas (usually, the state covers too much territory), but the machinery exists; and, moreover, state governments, in our constitutional system, have very broad powers. In short, the states are the best regional governments we have, and may be the best we are likely to get. Increasingly—but still far from adequately—the larger urban state governments are assuming new regional functions, in addition to their traditional preoccupation with highways, higher education, mental hospitals, and prisons. The newer urban-oriented functions include direct action and grants for housing, urban transportation, water supply and quality, and parks in urban areas, all truly regional activities. These responsibilities have been assumed in response to political pressures, not academic theorizing. But the fact that there has been a response indicates that the state governments are capable of acting on regional problems.

Governmental restructuring to cope better with spillovers would greatly change the fiscal scene, principally by substantially reducing local government responsibilities. A larger federal role in financing the public-benefit aspect of the schools, combined with the probable increase in the state role

TABLE 8-3   *Sources of Funds for Civilian Public Expenditure, Actual 1970-1971, and under Hypothetical Restructuring, by Level of Government*

Level of Government	Expenditure Class[a]				
	Economic Stabili- zation	Income Redis- tribution	Public Schools	Resource Allocation	Totals
Actual 1970-1971					
Federal	55%	75%	10%	34%	44%
State	45	15	39	30	28
Local	0	10	51	36	28
All Levels	100	100	100	100	100
Hypothetical[b]					
Federal	100	90	25	32	53
State	0	7	55	40	30
Local	0	3	20	28	17
All Levels	100	100	100	100	100

[a]Classifications are those explained in Table 8-1.
[b]On the basis of the restructuring outlined in the text.

to achieve the intrastate equalization the courts may require in future years, which will be discussed shortly, should substantially reduce local tax responsibility for this activity. Full federal financing of the redistributive services would reduce both local and state tax costs. Regionalization, through the state government or otherwise, would further reduce the local government role, but increase that of the state governments. On balance, the revenue needs of state governments might increase slightly, while the needs of the local governments might decline as much as 40 percent, under the proposals developed here. Table 8-3 illustrates this.

FISCAL DISPARITIES AND IMBALANCES

More federal responsibility for the financing of education and the redistributive activities would surely reduce fiscal disparities (especially between central cities and suburbs) and would help correct the fiscal imbalance among the levels of government. But it would not end the problem, especially for the state governments.

One way to deal with the continuing imbalance among the levels of government is for the federal government to share its revenues with the states, and with the local governments as well. A start on this has been made, in the form of the revenue-sharing legislation sponsored by President Nixon and enacted by Congress in late 1972. It provides for the sharing of $30 billion of federal revenue over a five-year period, on the basis of a formula that reflects mainly population and differential state-local tax-raising efforts. In essence, the federal government is now using its superior tax-raising capabilities to collect revenue on behalf of the lower levels of government. The success of the revenue-sharing proposal reflects the fact that the federal government has been able to carry on both its defense and its civilian programs with tax rates that are on balance substantially *lower* than they were fifteen or twenty years ago, while the state and local governments have been continually increasing tax rates.[4]

Revenue-sharing could facilitate the restructuring suggested above, because the increased responsibilities of state governments require such a new fiscal resource, especially in the large urban states with high tax effort that are even now aggressively coping with regional problems—states like Cali-

4. On a nationwide basis, state government income and sales tax rates in 1967 averaged 2.7 times those in effect in 1950. Advisory Commission on Intergovernmental Relations, *Sources of Increased State Collections: Economic Growth vs. Political Choice,* 1968.

fornia and New York. Indeed, with the proposed restructuring, they would need the funds more than the local governments, at present the most hard-pressed of the levels of government.

The cities initially objected to revenue-sharing proposals in the 1960s, because of their fear of being "shortchanged" by the states. A good case can be made that existing state grant programs do not adequately deal with the large cities. In the main, this is not a consequence of conscious discrimination, although in the past, rural-dominated legislatures have been discriminatory in the distribution of state aid. Most of the alleged shortchanging has been a consequence of the types of programs the states traditionally aid heavily. Much of state aid is for schools and highways. Schools and roads are ubiquitous, not just confined to the big cities, and many rural areas have much less taxable income and wealth per capita or per pupil than do the large cities; it is logical that the rural areas should be disproportionately aided for schools and roads.

There *is* one element of largely inadvertent discrimination against the cities in the typical state school-aid formulas. Usually, state aid programs are based on the numbers of school children and the local property-tax base per pupil. Big cities tend to have fewer school children per household in public schools than is the case in other parts of a given state; they also tend to have relatively high business-property values. Therefore, they appear to have low needs and high resources, and so they get little state aid for schools.

The difficulty with this is that the typical formula falsely assumes that the cost of providing a given quality of education is uniform throughout a state. But the evidence suggests that to provide an education equivalent in quality to that received in the better suburban schools would cost enormously more per pupil in the slum schools in the big cities.[5] Ideally, this should be resolved as part of the federal assumption of all the costs of the redistributive services, because the problem relates to low-income families. State aid is unlikely to be forthcoming in amounts large enough to permit school systems in big cities to provide schooling that is really equivalent to that in the better suburban schools.

Shifts in program responsibilities, expansion of state and federal aid, and federal revenue sharing combined would provide us with a set of fiscal institutions adequate to cope with the responsibilities of government in urban areas. But, aside from revenue sharing, none of these reforms can be achieved quickly, and some of them perhaps never. Meanwhile, urban local governments must function and raise money to do so. Although the defects of local revenue devices will necessarily be major ones as long as there is such heavy reliance on them, are there ways to improve the revenue-raising mechanisms local governments use?

Charges for Public Services

Not all of the difference between local government expenditure and the amounts received from the federal and state governments need be raised by taxation. Substantial amounts are presently raised from charges paid by the users of public services. Hospital charges and rents from public housing defray about 20 percent of local outlays for the redistributive activities, and miscellaneous school fees pay about 5 percent

---

5. A careful analysis of such cost differentials can be found in Betsy Levin, Thomas Muller, and Corazon Sandoval, *The Cities and the Equal Dollar Principal: An Analysis of the Purchasing Power of the Educational Dollar in Central City, Suburban, and Rural School Districts* (Washington, D.C.: The Urban Institute, 1973).

of the costs of the public schools (see Table 8-4). User charges amount to nearly 30 percent of outlays for the resource-allocation activities. For example, over 75 percent of the locally financed share of outlays for water supply and water quality come from user charges. A similar percentage applies to outlays for transportation (except highways).

TABLE 8-4 *The Financing of Local Government Expenditure, 1970-1971 (In Billions of Dollars)*

Financing	Income Redistribution	Public Schools	Resource Allocation	Totals
	Expenditure Class[a]			
Total Local Government Direct Expenditure	16.0	41.3	45.8	103.1
Financed by:				
Federal and State Aid	7.9	20.2	9.1[b]	37.2
User Charges	3.2	2.1	12.6	17.9
Residual (From Taxes, Borrowing, Miscellaneous Minor Receipts)	4.9	19.0	24.1	48.0

Source: Adapted from U.S. Census Bureau, *Governmental Finances in 1970-71* (1972).
[a]Classifications are those explained in Table 8-1.
[b]Includes state aid for general local government support.

Roughly 20 percent of the local costs of refuse collection and of highways is met from user charges.

But why *should* governments charge for public services? Is there not a contradiction in terms between a service provided *publicly* and a charge for its use? Surely, governments are providing services precisely because the private sector, where prices *are* charged for services, is not believed to do an adequate job in certain areas.

There are some conditions clearly limiting the use of charges or prices for services in the public sector. It is obviously inappropriate to charge the poor for their consumption of public services designed explicitly to benefit them as such; we cannot redistribute income in money or in the form of services by making the poor pay back the amounts redistributed. Thus user charges for most health and welfare services and tuition for the public schools would be preposterous ways of financing these public services.

Another general situation in which user charges are inappropriate refers to what economic theorists have defined as a "pure public good." This is a service whose dominant characteristic is that no one can be denied the benefits from the service, regardless of whether or not he pays for it. Such a service must be provided by governments, rather than by private enterprises; no rational person would willingly pay a private firm for a service if he could enjoy the service without paying for it. Examples include national defense, the maintenance of public safety, the visual attractiveness provided by open space, control of communicable diseases, and the cleaning and lighting of streets. In all such cases, not only is it impossible to exclude the nonpayer, but also one person's enjoyment of the benefits does not in any way deny these benefits to others.

Most public services are not pure public goods. The exclusion principle does apply at least in part, and use of the service by one person does deny it to others. Thus, user charges are feasible, but not necessarily desirable. As noted above, they are not appropriate for redistributive services. They are also of limited applicability where the service produces substantial public benefits, aside from those enjoyed by the user as such. For example, libraries could be financed on a charge basis, but tax support can be justified on the grounds that libraries serve an educational function with external (to the user) benefits, and therefore potential users unwilling to

pay the charges should be encouraged to use the service anyhow. Similarly, it was argued in Chapter 7 that public transportation systems may produce significant external benefits
and, if so, should be subsidized from tax revenues.

Even where there are substantial external benefits, the possible application of user charges need not be rejected out of
hand. User charges may be, and often are, appropriate to
finance that portion of the costs of the services reflecting
private benefits, that is, benefits to the users themselves.
Where the exclusion principle applies, either the supply of
services must be continually expanded to accommodate all
those who wish to use the service or there must be some basis
for apportioning the limited quantity of the service among
competing users. If the service is free and in limited supply, it
will be apportioned by congestion or by queuing up. If there
is a charge, the rationing will be by price. As the earlier discussion of pricing in transportation suggested, there are some
real disadvantages in nonprice rationing in a society in which
most goods and services are rationed on the basis of price.

There are many instances in which the supply of public
services cannot be readily expanded, at least in the short run,
and therefore some system of rationing is necessary. For
example, the expansion of water supply capacity has a very
long gestation period. While capacity is being expanded,
droughts can produce severe water shortages. Because Americans consume water for all sorts of optional purposes above
and beyond basic bodily and sanitary needs, it is entirely
possible to increase water charges to encourage reductions in
water consumption, such as reduced lawn sprinkling. The conventional alternative is the use of legal restrictions that are
hard to enforce and that to some extent, therefore, amount to
a tax on public-spiritedness.

In some circumstances, it is difficult to expand the supply

even in the long run, usually because the external costs are so high. Examples include urban expressways oriented toward the central business district (CBD) (see Chapter 7) and the capacity of CBD surface streets. The use of the facilities must then be limited. To allow it to be done by congestion is to reduce the economic value of the facility for *all* users, because a major purpose of investment in transportation is to reduce travel time.

It is often objected that rationing by price is especially hard on low-income people. As we have seen, this is not always the case. Often the heavy users of public facilities suitable for pricing are not the poor. The poor do not drive cars to work in the CBD, nor do they have large lawns to water; they tend not to be users of golf courses, or the predominant consumers of higher education. When such services are subsidized, middle-income households are often being subsidized from taxes paid in good measure by low-income people.

Moreover, if there are alternatives to the service for which a high price is being charged, it is difficult to agree that the poor are really being heavily burdened. Finally, there are much better ways to help the poor than by failing to charge adequately for services they consume in minuscule quantities.

In addition to rationing, user charges can serve another important function. Prices and the demand for services at various prices provide guidelines for decisions on public investment. If the external benefits are modest, as is probably true for highways and water supply, for example, governments are in effect acting as agents for users. Their function is to provide the quantity and quality of services users want. But given the fact that resources used for highways or water supply or anything else cannot be used for other worthy purposes, what users want can be rationally defined only in terms of what they are willing to pay for the service. If user charges are employed, public agencies will know how highly the service is valued by users.

It cannot be assumed that user demand is insensitive to price variations. Like most other things, the situation is not a yes-or-no one. Consider one example in the water-supply field. There is some cost to repairing leaking faucets, a cost that building owners must bear. Leaking faucets consume a great deal of water; repair of leaks can significantly reduce water consumption and the demand for new water-supply capacity. At some level of water charges, it will be advantageous for users to pay to repair leaks in return for lower water bills. If the water charges are set at very low levels, a public decision to expand system capacity, made necessary by the losses due to leakage, seems a highly wasteful use of resources.

One attractive feature of user charges is that they can overcome the problem of geographic spillovers of benefits. A public agency can tax only those people, sales, or property within its geographic jurisdiction; it cannot tax outsiders who may be benefiting from the public services it provides. However, if it employs user charges, it is recouping costs from the users who benefit, wherever they reside, if in fact they use the service. Thus gross undersupply of public services by local governments is less likely with user-charge financing than with tax financing.

The case for user charges, therefore, rests mainly on their capacity to improve decision making regarding the supply of public services and the allocation of the services among users. As devices for raising money pure and simple, user charges have few merits compared to general taxation. Nevertheless, urban governments can expand their revenues by more intensive employment of user charges, where appropriate. User charges currently are often not applied where they make sense, and they are often badly applied.

For example, there is substantial tax, rather than user-charge, financing of air- and water-pollution control. Yet it is fairly easy to identify the specific actions that give rise to public costs. The benefits of air- and water-pollution control are highly diffused, but the sources of the public costs are very much individual, identifiable ones—the polluters themselves. Moreover, it is possible to apply charges that are related to the quantity and quality of the effluent, as has been done in the Ruhr Basin with respect to water pollution for many years. The collection and disposal of solid waste are similarly suitable for user charges, as is fire protection. Most local government highway expenditure is tax financed, which need not be the case.

Transportation services provide striking illustrations of the inept application of user charges—the flat transit fare, poor charging for on-street parking, and most of all, gasoline and license taxes for highways. These taxes have some relation to the amount of use of the highways by all users and by individual users over long periods of time. But flat charges of this kind cannot possibly discourage people from freely using the very high-cost roads at the very high-cost periods. There are many similar, though lesser, examples, particularly connected with the common municipal practice of issuing annual permits, for a fee, for the use of public facilities, like recreational facilities. Once the permit is issued, each use is free to the consumer. The occasional user at uncrowded hours may be discouraged by the cost of the permit fee, but the permit-holder has no incentive to avoid the crowded hours. Indeed, he can lower his cost per use by using the facility as often as possible. Therefore, permits are likely to be bought only by frequent users.

The Property Tax

No matter how widely and efficiently user charges are employed, local general taxes will remain a major source of funds for public services, especially if intergovernmental fiscal arrangements continue along existing lines. The dominant local tax, producing 85 percent of local-government tax revenues, is the property tax. There are nearly 66,000 local government units using the property tax, about 18,000 of them in metropolitan areas, with diverse tax bases, tax rates, and expenditure needs. The tax finances the overwhelming bulk of the local share of school costs and a major fraction of the local share of most other government activities.

The property tax suffers from numerous disabilities. The disadvantages might not be serious if the tax were a minor one, imposed at low rates. But it is not minor. In urban areas outside the South, bills for property taxes typically average more than 2 percent of the *market* value of taxable property and in the large central cities, particularly in the Northeast, rates in excess of 3 percent are not uncommon. This may not sound high, although it is by historic standards. However, property taxes in the large urban states are equivalent, in revenue yield, to a flat-rate tax on personal income (after personal exemptions) of 10 percent or more. Some of the disadvantages of the property tax are inherent in the tax itself. Others stem from its use by so many small local government units within a single metropolitan area, and might be mitigated if the tax were imposed at uniform rates over wider geographic areas, such as whole counties.

In the discussion of policies affecting urban housing in Chapter 4, two of the most serious difficulties with the property tax were discussed at some length. One is its deterrent effects on the consumption of housing, largely a problem of

central cities. To recapitulate, the tax amounts to high percentages of annual housing costs to consumers. Considered as
a sales tax, its rates in urban areas are equivalent to a sales
tax of 25 percent or more, far higher than the sales or excise
tax rates applied to most other forms of consumer expenditure. For homeowners, especially well-to-do ones, the tax is
offset by federal income tax advantages. Moreover, the property tax on suburban housing is clearly linked to the services
it finances. But renters have no offset and in central cities the
link between the property tax and public services is a very
obscure one. The property tax in central cities, therefore,
imposes a serious impediment to the needed rebuilding of the
central-city housing stock, an impediment that is increasing,
not decreasing, with time, as property-tax rates rise. There is
much evidence that, in the large central cities, these rates
have been climbing steeply during the past decade.

A second difficulty discussed in Chapter 4 is the incentive
that heavy reliance on the property tax creates for "fiscal
zoning"—the control of land use to maximize the tax base of
each of the many small suburban governmental units and to
minimize public expenditure requirements. The latter is done
by zoning out moderate-income families likely to have large
numbers of public school children, principally by requiring
large minimum-lot-sizes. This raises land costs for housing
in a metropolitan area. It also leads to a highly dispersed
development pattern with increased transportation and utility
costs.

Fiscal zoning is unlikely to eliminate disparities in property-tax bases among local government units. Indeed, its
frequent effect is to reinforce them and to further enhance the
fiscal position of the community with large amounts of taxable
property per resident or per pupil. One consequence is the
effect on the choice of location within a metropolitan area.

Clearly, one would prefer to live in a community able to provide very generous services per dollar of property tax paid by a resident; the prices of houses may be higher in such a community, but not as much higher as the property tax advantage would suggest.

Also, there is an impact on the choice of location by businesses. Firms are not likely to move long distances in response to local tax differentials, for differentials in other business costs are much more important. However, within a metropolitan area, these other business costs tend to be similar in many alternative locations. Wage rates, water and energy costs, and costs of transportation of raw materials and finished products do not vary greatly within a metropolitan area. Thus, tax differentials may be the *only* significant cost differentials, and some firms will respond to these differentials by moving to the low-tax jurisdiction, further enhancing its fiscal advantages.

One general effect of this is to discourage communities from increasing tax rates to finance improvements in public services, lest they discourage industry from locating there.[6] Another effect, found less frequently, is that the business property-tax base located in low-tax places with few school children is effectively sterilized for school-tax purposes. In the extreme cases, where there are industrial enclaves with few residents, the industrial property is in effect tax exempt for school purposes.

Local tax differentials can also reinforce the one situation

---

6. It is often asserted that this will not occur, because industry is sensitive to differences in public service levels. This may be true among regions, but probably is not true within a single metropolitan area. The principal property-tax-financed service is education; a firm's employees can live in an adjacent high-tax community with good schools, while the plant is located in a low-tax community with poor ones.

in which other business costs do vary significantly within metropolitan areas. For many kinds of goods-handling activities, the central cities have serious cost disadvantages, with regard to land availability and congestion. Major local tax differentials can accelerate the migration from the central city to outlying areas. In the Northeast, such tax differentials in favor of the suburbs, are frequent. For example, the older cities in New Jersey have property-tax rates that are two or more times as high as those in the outlying areas.

Clearly, both the pressures for fiscal zoning and the locational effects of property-tax disparities are not inherent in the property tax, but are a consequence of the fragmented structure of local governments in most large metropolitan areas. If area-wide taxes were used, for example to finance education (which absorbs over half of all property-tax revenue), these deficiencies might disappear. They would also disappear if nearly all school costs were financed by statewide property taxation, as has been proposed by governors and special commissions in an increasing number of states, such as California, Michigan, New Jersey, and New York. Any wholesale shift in school financing to the states or to the federal government would work in this direction.

Proposals for statewide property taxation for the schools, or other types of domestic overhauling of, and increases in, state financing of the schools are in part responses to the political perception that local property taxes are decidedly unpopular,[7] and in part efforts to deal with the fiscal-zoning problem. But, more generally, such proposals reflect concern over the very considerable degree of inequality among school

---

7. A survey made in early 1972 indicates that Americans believe the property tax to be the "most unfair tax" in our fiscal system. Advisory Commission on Intergovernmental Relations, *Public Opinion and Taxes* (May 1972).

districts in the amount of fiscal resources per pupil that is the case in most American states. Typically, the richer school districts within a state are able to spend substantially more per pupil, while maintaining low property-tax rates, than are the poorer school districts, despite the existence of large state school-aid programs. Table 8-5 shows the data for the state of Connecticut in 1970–1971; it is by no means unusual or extreme.[8]

TABLE 8-5 *Financing of Schools by Property Taxes: Rich Towns versus Poor Towns, Connecticut, 1970-1971*

	Net Current Expenditure per Pupil	School Tax as Percent of Market Value of Property
Fifty Richest Towns	$989	1.1
Fifty Poorest Towns	732	1.9

In a series of court cases, such disparities have been widely challenged as unconstitutional failures to treat the residents of a state equally. Although the U.S. Supreme Court held in March 1973 that the conventional system of school financing is not a violation of the U.S. Constitution (but rather a matter of bad public policy to be resolved by legislatures), at least two state supreme courts (in California and New Jersey) have found the system to violate the state's own constitution. The threats of court action, combined with the widespread agree-

---

8. State of Connecticut, *Report of the Governor's Commission on Tax Reform,* vol. 3 *Local Government: Schools and Property* (Hartford, December 1972), p. 55. In Connecticut in 1970–1971, local governments financed 64 percent of the costs of the schools, as compared to 51 percent nationwide (see Table 8-3); on the other hand, the disparities in property value per pupil among the districts in Connecticut are much less than in most other states with higher state-aid percentages.

ment by liberals and conservatives alike[9] that so much inequality is obnoxious, make it likely that major equalizing reforms in the property-tax method of school financing will be common among the states during the 1970s.

Some of the defects in a property tax levied at high rates are said to be inherent, rather than correctable. One such allegation concerns the regressivity of the property tax. The property tax as it exists today appears to be the most regressive of the major forms of taxation used in the United States. That is, its burden, as a percentage of income, is much higher for low-income people than it is for high-income people. This is principally because housing is so large a component of consumer spending for low-income families. This is less true on a lifetime basis (for example, many elderly low-income people live in housing acquired years earlier when their incomes were higher), but at any given moment the property tax is decidedly regressive.

It is true that if the property tax were applied at a uniformly nationwide rate to all forms of capital and were uniformly administered, it would not be regressive at all. Rather, it would be borne by the owners of capital in proportion to their holdings and would be a progressive tax, because ownership of wealth increases rapidly as income rises. But that is not the kind of tax we have, or could ever have, as long as the tax is a local one. Where the tax rate is high relative to the average tax imposed on *all* capital (regardless of form, ownership, or location), the economic burden can be shifted from owners of capital to the users of the taxed facilities, that is, the occupants of buildings and the consumer of goods and services produced in buildings. If the tax is shifted, then its regressivity

---

9. The Connecticut commission was a very conservative group, but was deeply concerned with inequality.

depends upon how the tax is administered and the income elasticity of the demand for the services produced by taxed facilities, notably housing. As noted in Chapter 4, the long-term elasticity of demand for housing appears to be below 1.0 for renters and above 1.0 for owner-occupants, in large part no doubt because of the income tax advantages of home ownership.

Now property-tax rates tend to be high in central cities, where there are many renters and low-income homeowners, who should not be expected to have high income elasticities (because they cannot profit much from the income tax advantages).[10] Tax rates are also high in moderate-income suburbs, where elasticities should likewise be low. Thus the property tax on housing on balance is in practice very regressive indeed among, say, all the residents of a given state or of the country as a whole. Data that directly compare property taxes paid by homeowners with their incomes, from the 1960 and 1970 Census of Housing, bear this out. For example, in 1971, the property tax on owner-occupied single-family houses averaged 4.9 percent of family income for the entire United States, but was twice that high for the homeowners with the lowest incomes; in contrast, it was 3.7 percent or less for those with incomes above $10,000.

Another inherent difficulty is in connection with administration of the tax, that is, assessment of individual properties for tax purposes. The true value of a parcel of real property

---

10. It has been pointed out that the value of rental housing is a higher multiple of rents as rent increases and that this should tend to make a shifted property tax on rental housing progressive, even if the income elasticity of demand is fairly low. However, the customary way of assessing the value of rental housing is to multiply the rent rolls by a uniform multiplier, not one that varies directly with the level of rent. As long as this is the case, the tax on rental housing in a high-tax-rate jurisdiction will be a regressive one.

is known only at the time that the property changes hands in a market sale in which both buyer and seller are willing and knowledgeable. At other times, assessors must guess at values by looking at recent sales of similar property, or the income produced by the property, or the cost of constructing a similar building. Because each piece of real property is unique, at least in its location, it is not surprising that the best assessors can do is to come reasonably close,[11] especially in large central cities, where the differences among individual properties are very complex. This produces substantial inequities among individuals and hostility to the tax itself.

In view of all the defects of the property tax, why does it persist? In fact, it does more than persist; in recent years the percentage increase in property tax collections has been far greater than the percentage increase in gross national product. The fact that it does produce so much money is one reason why it persists. A second reason is that it is the only major tax reserved to the local governments, with income and payroll taxes heavily used by the federal government and sales taxes heavily used by the states. Local governments apparently feel more free to impose heavy property taxes than to add to state sales taxes or to impose high income-tax rates, on top of federal and, in most places, state income taxes. In reality, this suggests an illusion—a greater willingness by taxpayers to part with money when labeled in one way, than to part with the same amount of money when labeled in another.

The fact that real property is visible and can be discovered readily makes the tax more suitable for administration, however inadequately, by small local governments than, say, in-

---

11. In contrast, someone's income or a store's retail sales are objectively ascertainable quantities, although they may be hard for the tax collector to discover.

come taxes. Another aspect of the administrative problem relates to the existence of "layers" of local government existing in the same area: counties, municipalities, townships, school districts, and special-purpose units. In the Chicago area, for example, there are more than 1,000 local units with property-taxing powers. The layers do not have boundaries that coincide in most cases, so that the residents of a community may be in different combinations of townships, school districts, and special districts. It is not hard to compute total property-tax liability for all these layers, because the real property itself has a geographic identity. To compute income-tax liability for thousands of possible combinations would be far more difficult.

Land-Value Taxation

It is clear that, aside from its revenue productivity, the positive attributes of the property tax are insignificant compared to its defects. There is one form of property taxation, however, for which an entirely different, and favorable, balance of advantages and disadvantages can be struck. This is the taxation of the value of bare sites—the land alone, without any tax on the building on the site—an old idea vigorously espoused by Henry George a century ago. The land-value tax is the economist's ideal: it is equitable; it is neutral in its economic effects; and it is positively desirable as a replacement for the conventional property tax with its many bad economic effects.

The argument for land-value taxation, on equity grounds, is that most of the value of land is a consequence of investment in public facilities and utilities, community development, and population growth, not a result of action by individual owners. The owners realize large increases in land values over time, increments that they do not earn by their own efforts. It is fair, therefore, that the community recapture these "un-earned increments" by taxation and then use them for public purposes.

Land-value taxation is economically neutral in the sense that it does not change land-use incentives, compared to no tax at all, because changing the use of the land does not affect tax liability. The most profitable possible use of the site before the tax is imposed continues to be the most profitable use. But the present property tax, applying to both land and buildings, is not neutral. The construction of a bigger or better building, or improvement of an existing building, increases tax liability. Therefore, the present tax tends to discourage investment in buildings.

A switch to exclusive taxation of land (or to heavy taxes on land and light taxes on buildings) could have strong positive effects, by removing the disincentive to invest in buildings. Owners would be encouraged to develop sites more intensively, thereby securing a flow of income from which to pay the land-value tax. It is likely that a switch to land-value taxation would encourage development most in two parts of a metropolitan area—in the central sections, on valuable sites where older and smaller buildings are now standing, and on the urban-rural fringe where landowners would be less likely to hold out for future speculative gains. Landowners would generally be under pressure to better utilize their land or to sell out to others willing and able to better use the site.

Heavy or exclusive taxation of land values is widely practiced—in western Canada, Australia, and New Zealand, for example. There is a renewed interest among economists, planners, and public officials in land-value taxation for the United States. In part, this renewed interest is based on a closer scrutiny of some of the alleged defects. It has been argued that land values are not large enough to permit a complete replacement of the conventional property tax by the land-value tax. It has also been argued that there are serious administrative problems.

The experience elsewhere suggests that the latter argument is invalid. In fact, it appears that assessment of land values may be easier to carry out than assessment of land and buildings combined. In regard to the former argument, a recent study indicates that 40 percent of the market value of taxable real property is accounted for by the land alone, and that land values have been rising at about three times the rate of increase in the general price level.[12] If this is so, a land-value tax at rates averaging no more than 6 percent nationwide would be sufficient to replace the entire present tax on land and buildings.

The very rapid rate of increase in land values in recent years makes this even more attractive, for it indicates that huge "unearned increments" have been accruing to landowners. Moreover, landowners tend to have relatively high incomes, a consequence of income tax, mortgage market, and other conditions. There is poetic justice in heavy land-value taxation: at present, land is typically taxed at rates, relative to market value, that are less than half those applied to buildings. We now, perversely, favor the speculator who impedes development and discourage the investor in new and better buildings.

Local Nonproperty Taxes

Outside the English-speaking world, local government is relatively unimportant, but it does exist and does raise significant amounts of tax revenue in many countries, especially

---

12. Allen D. Manvel, "Trends in the Value of Real Estate and Land, 1956 to 1966," in *Three Land Research Studies,* National Commission on Urban Problems, Research Report no. 12, 1968.

in Western Europe. And unlike the English-speaking countries, the taxes used are mainly *not* on land and buildings, but on income, sales, or business activity. Thus, the existence of local government does not necessarily require heavy reliance on property taxation, although such is the case in the United States.

Less than one-sixth of the tax revenue of American local governments come from local nonproperty taxes, such as income and sales taxes, excises on public utilities, liquor, cigarettes, and gasoline, and a variety of revenue-raising license taxes. This is, however, a deceptive figure for two reasons. First, some types of local governments, especially school districts and county governments, hardly use the nonproperty taxes at all; they are largely the province of municipal governments.[13] Second, local nonproperty taxes are not used in some parts of the country. General sales and income taxes, the most productive sources, were not used by local governments in twenty of the fifty states as of early 1972.

General sales taxes are used by local governments in twenty-five states; local income taxes are widely used in five states and by a small number of large cities in four others. With few exceptions, the very large cities use either sales or income taxes; New York City uses both. The forty-eight largest cities combined get about 40 percent of their tax revenues from local nonproperty taxes. In some of them, the local nonproperty taxes exceed the property tax in importance.

In some respects, the nonproperty taxes can overcome the disadvantages of the property tax. For one thing, they do not

---

13. One implication of this is that nonproperty taxes contribute little to the financing of schools or of the functions in which the counties play a large role, like welfare. However, there is a trend toward increasing the use of these taxes by county governments.

have the unfortunate effects on housing consumption that characterize the property tax in central cities. For another, they can be a lot less regressive than the property tax. Even without graduated rates, an income tax can be made mildly progressive in its incidence, if personal exemptions are permitted, as is done in Michigan cities. Usually, however, there are no exemptions, and often property income (interest, dividends, and rents) is not taxed. This makes a local income tax somewhat regressive, but less so than the property tax.

The sales tax is frequently denounced as a highly regressive one, but this need not be the case. In fact, if food is exempt from the tax, as it is in some states, the tax is more or less proportional to income. This is because food and housing (exempt from sales taxation in general) absorb high percentages of the incomes of low-income people. However, even if food is taxed, the sales tax is less regressive than the housing component of the property tax.

Another advantage of the nonproperty taxes is that they can enable the central city to tap the wider tax-paying capacity of the metropolitan economy, by taxing sales to visitors and non-resident shoppers and, more important, by taxing the income earned by suburban residents in the central city. It should be noted, however, that there is some inequity in this. The central city has a fiscal claim on the whole metropolitan economy largely because of its services to the poor of the area who are concentrated in the central city. Ideally, all suburbanites, not just those who happen to work in the central city, should help defray the costs of these services. The commuters can be reached by the city's income tax; other suburbanites cannot. This solution then is expedient, if somewhat inequitable.

Nonproperty taxes, however, do share some disadvantages with the property tax. They too can have adverse effects on the location of economic activity, if tax rates are much higher in one location in a metropolitan area than in others. There is one rather striking example of this. Prior to 1965, New York City was a sales-tax island, for there was no sales tax in either adjacent New Jersey or in the surrounding suburban counties in New York State. A careful economic study indicated that the city's sales tax (then 4 percent), by itself, was responsible for the diversion of nearly 25 percent of the city's retail sales of house furnishings and apparel to suburban areas.[14] This in turn had serious effects on employment in retail establishments.

Also, local nonproperty taxes do not eliminate the problem of disparities in fiscal resources, although they mitigate this problem for the central city. Just as real property is unequally distributed among suburban communities, so also are retail sales and personal income. For example, the community with a large regional shopping center could finance all its expenditure from a moderate sales tax, but its immediate neighbors might have only negligible sales-tax receipts. A rich residential community would have a very ample base for a personal income tax, while its poorer neighboring residential communities might require exceedingly high income-tax rates to finance their required public expenditures.

In summary, local nonproperty taxes appear to be a second-best solution, useful mainly for large central cities. Until and unless intergovernmental fiscal arrangements are changed, the cities must do something to finance their requirements. The nonproperty taxes are, on balance, superior to further increases in the conventional property tax.

---

14. See Henry M. Levin, "An Analysis of the Economic Effects of the New York City Sales Tax," in *Financing Government in New York City,* New York University Graduate School of Public Administration (New York, 1966), pp. 635–692.

Conclusion

Fiscal conditions in urban America have been changing very rapidly indeed in recent years. Since the first edition of this book was written, rapidly rising unit costs have shown dramatically how vulnerable labor-intensive urban governments are to inflation. Unionization of public employees has proceeded rapidly, and the unions have become much more militant, more like their private-sector counterparts. Strikes in local government, which averaged fewer than 30 a year before 1966, rose to nearly 400 in 1969 and again in 1970, and, not surprisingly, local government employees in the larger cities now have salaries and fringe benefits that are well in excess of those enjoyed by comparable workers in the private sector.[15] And, in the last few years, taxpayer revolts—in the form of voter rejections of proposed bond issues, school budgets, and tax-rate increases—have become far more common.

On the other hand, the enactment of federal revenue sharing, the slowing down in the rate of population increase, declines in school enrollments, and the greater reliance of the state-local sector on taxes (especially the personal income tax) whose revenues grow rapidly with economic expansion seem about to produce real fiscal ease for many state and local governments. Projections for the years immediately ahead indicate sizable fiscal surpluses for the state-local sector as a whole, even though comparable projections made in the 1960s indicated large fiscal deficits. However, the fiscal ease is likely to be very uneven. In particular, the prospects for large central cities remain grim and those for moderate-income suburbs only slightly less so, while those for state governments and

---

15. See Charles L. Schultze, Edward R. Fried, Alice M. Rivlin, and Nancy H. Teeters, *Setting National Priorities: the 1973 Budget* (Washington, D.C.: The Brookings Institution, 1972), pp. 298–299.

affluent suburbs are generally rosy. The reforms discussed here are framed largely in the light of the prospects for the central cities.

In criticizing existing fiscal institutions and discussing possible reforms—changes in intergovernmental fiscal relations that produce a greater role for the federal and state governments; greater and more sophisticated applications of user charges; deemphasis of the conventional property tax and heavier taxation of land values—this chapter is not a quest for reduced taxes for individual taxpayers or the permanent resolution of fiscal conflicts in urban America. In fact, a greater role for higher-level governments is likely to lead to more public expenditure and thus higher, not lower, taxes, on a combined federal, state, and local basis. If tax rates are rising, fiscal conflict will persist.

Instead, the goal has been to explore ways to help governments serving urban areas perform the functions that only governments can do, along two lines: through an improved framework for decision making on public expenditure (handling spillovers properly and using the signals given by the price system, in the form of user charges, to help guide public investment policy) and through the use of revenue sources with few toxic side effects on housing, urban form, location of economic activity, and income distribution. Other specific reform proposals no doubt also satisfy these criteria; the purpose of the chapter has not been to advocate a particular set of fiscal policies, but to illustrate the application of economic reasoning to the problems of financing urban government.

That, of course, describes the purpose of this book in general. A large number of policy alternatives have been reviewed; in many cases, the appraisal has been a favorable one. In some cases, the appraisal has been so favorable that phrases connoting a moral imperative, like "should be done" and "must be done," have been used. However, these are just one

economist's findings. The book will have fulfilled its mission
if it has succeeded in providing the reader with a different
perspective on urban problems, that of the economist, and
even more if it has stimulated the reader to challenge the
reasoning that lies behind the policy findings. But in making
the challenge, please keep in mind a few of the key elements
of economics: the need for choosing the best among many
desirable end results; the importance of finding the most efficient means for achieving those ends; and the prevalence of
interdependency, that is, the external effects that are ever
present in public affairs. Remember that resources used for
one purpose are not available for others; money is not real,
but labor, land, buildings, and machinery are; it is usually
desirable to enjoy benefits now and incur costs later; and indirect ways of achieving goals have resource costs just as direct
ways do.

Perhaps the most frequently overlooked and most insistently
urged analytical argument of the book is this: existing institutions and policies have negative, as well as positive, economic
effects on the resolution of urban problems. The mitigation of
the harmful effects, by revising existing institutions, may be
more important than any conceivable combination of glamor-
ous and wholly new institutions, policies, and mechanisms.
This is hardly a revolutionary prescription, but we should remember that, despite all the shortcomings, the economic record
of the United States, Canada, Japan, and Western Europe has
been one of success, not failure, since the end of World War
II, with high and rising standards of living and elimination of
the scourge of mass unemployment and destitution. Societies
with economic arrangements that, while paying serious attention to environmental difficulties, make likely the achievement
of universal affluence within another generation must be doing something right.

Index

Aaron, Henry J., 146
Accessibility: "bid-rent" model of, 13–17; land values and, 17–18; measurement of, 10–11, 12
Agglomeration economies, 22
Air pollution, 174 (*see also* Pollution; Quality of environment); assimilative capacity of environment and, 176–177; charging polluters for, 247; control problems for, 5, 180; costs of removing, 187–188; graduated tax on, 186; higher proportions of income for elimination of, 54–55; incineration and, 181; spillover and, 236; transportation and, 198
Alonso, William, 13
Apartments (*see* Public housing; Rental housing)
Arrow, Kenneth, 27
Automobiles: central-city poor and, 217–218; decentralization and, 49, 53; "highway bias" in public policy and, 192–198; public transportation and, 189–192; taxes on use of, 186

Baltimore, 141, 142, 231
Berkeley, 138

"Bid-rent" model, 13–17
Biochemical oxygen demand (BOD), 178, 179, 185–186
Blacks: automobile ownership among, 62; European immigrants compared with, 39–41; migration to cities by, 34–35, 74; poverty among, 31, 34–41; racial composition of cities and, 35–36; small business ownership by, 75–76; substandard housing conditions of, 43; unemployment among, 74; urban renewal and, 114
Boston: historic sites in, 172; rail system in, 79, 105, 216; rent control in, 138; suburban employment of ghetto residents of, 79
Building codes, 101, 102, 128–129, 223
Bureau of Labor Statistics, 94, 146
Businesses: agglomeration economics and, 22; black ownership of, 75–76; changes in "centrality" for, 50; "trade-off" theory of location of, 10–12
Bus service, 217

Cab service, 218–219
California: home loan programs in,

265

Index